Serpentine Pavilion 2024 Archipelagic Void   Mass Studies

Edited by
Alexa Chow, Gonzalo Herrero Delicado
and Yesomi Umolu

Foreword

Serpentine's Foreword   2

Sponsor's Foreword   7

Serpentine Pavilions 2000–2023   8

Thank You   20

Project Team   23

Serpentine's Foreword

Leading his firm Mass Studies, Seoul-based South Korean architect Minsuk Cho is the twenty-third practitioner to accept the invitation to design the Serpentine Pavilion. Cho began his design process by investigating the history and form of previous commissions, asking what can be uncovered and added to the Serpentine site — a place that has already featured numerous iterations from a roster of great architects and artists. Tracing the size, shape and location of past Pavilions, his research led him to shift from the architectural focus of a singular structure situated at the centre to embracing the centre as an open space.

Titled *Archipelagic Void*, the 23rd Serpentine Pavilion pays homage to Édouard Glissant's archipelagic thinking, a rhizomatic interpretation of architecture that resonates with Cho's approach. Glissant states that: 'The purpose of architecture has always been to show, to claim a space, and the monument is proof of that. Perhaps in our world today, our archipelagic world of Relation and rhizomes, the basis and the role of architecture will no longer be to show the monument, but to show the invisible. The aesthetic of the invisible brings us back to the aesthetic of the void and the infinite, which need not produce anguish, but hope. That could be the new ambition of architecture.'[1]

Cho envisions the Pavilion as a unique void surrounded by a constellation of smaller, adaptable structures strategically positioned at the periphery of the lawn. These structures, aptly referred as 'islands' by Cho, are each unique in size, height and form. Built predominantly in timber, they are supported by identical footings that adapt to the slightly sloping topography of the site. The curving edges of the individual roofs are conjoined by a steel ring that forms an oculus in the centre, drawing natural light. Radiating from the circular void, these islands act as nodes in the lawn, reaching out to connect to Serpentine South and the pedestrian networks in the park. This layout also references traditional Korean houses that feature a *madang*, an open courtyard located at the centre. This space connects to various residential quarters, accommodating individual everyday activities and larger collective rituals throughout the changing seasons.

Around the void, each of the five 'islands' is conceived as a 'content machine', serving a

1. *The Archipelago Conversations*, Édouard Glissant and Hans Ulrich Obrist, isolarii, 2022 (Sixth Edition), p. 52.

2. Co-curated by Hou Hanru and Hans Ulrich Obrist, *Cities on the Move* is an exhibition that responded to the rapid urbanisation that took place in East and South East Asia in the late 20th century. Presenting the dynamic and highly creative situation of contemporary architecture, urban planning and visual culture in the region, the exhibition showcases works of more than 150 architects, artists, filmmakers and designers.

different purpose and individually named. The *Gallery* hosts a six-channel sound installation, presenting *The Willow Is* 〈버들은〉 during the summer and transitions to *Moonlight* 〈월정명〉 in autumn. Created by musician and composer Jang Young-Gyu, the work incorporates sounds from nature and human activities recorded in Kensington Gardens with traditional Korean vocal music and instruments to depict the transition of seasons. The largest structure of the five 'islands' is the *Auditorium*. With benches built into its inner walls, this space will provide an area for public gathering, performances and talks to take place. Located to the north is *The Library of Unread Books* by artist Heman Chong and archivist Renée Staal. This 'living' reference library, is comprised of donated unread books to form a pool of common knowledge, addressing notions of access, excess and the politics of distribution. The southeast *Play Tower* is a pyramid structure fitted with a bright orange netscape for children to climb and interact with. In a nod to the history of the Serpentine, Cho incorporates the *Tea House* to the east of the Pavilion. Designed by James Grey West, the Serpentine South building originally functioned as a teahouse before reopening as an art gallery in 1970.

This Pavilion is the outcome of almost thirty years of dialogue with Minsuk Cho. We first met Cho with Rem Koolhaas at OMA Rotterdam in 1996 during the research for the exhibition *Cities on the Move*.[2] In 1998, Cho moved to New York to establish Cho Slade Architecture with partner James Slade before returning to Korea to open his own practice Mass Studies in 2003. He conceived the practice as a critical investigation of architecture in the context of mass production and densely populated urban conditions. Instead of providing a solution based on a singular, unified perspective, Mass Studies focuses on exploring spatial systems, materials and techniques that respond to the complex conditions of the site. The aim is to foster new ways to connect their projects with the environment in which they are situated, creating spaces that bring people together. We were struck by the Won Buddhism Wonnam Temple which the Serpentine team visited in 2023. A central *madang* is also created in the Wonnam Temple for people to gather and stay, linking up the various spaces within the complex including the Inhyewon Donors Memorial to the south, the Main Sanctuary to the north, the Community Hall to the east and the Annex to the west. Working in close conversation with their neighbours, seven alleyways adjacent to the Wonnam Temple were configured and opened up to provide multiple access points for visitors. Mass Studies and Cho's ability to create daily encounters between people and architecture had been deeply impressive, something which is also well reflected in the design of this year's Pavilion.

The Serpentine Pavilion commission aims to offer audiences the first-hand opportunity to see and engage with the work of world-renowned architects in person. This pioneering commission, which began in 2000 with Zaha Hadid, has become an international site for architectural experimentation and has presented the first UK structures by some of the world's greatest architects. In recent years, it has grown into a highly anticipated showcase for emerging architectural talents, also featuring designs led by visual artists. Recent Pavilions include *À table* designed by Lina Ghotmeh — Architecture (2023); *Black Chapel* designed by Theaster Gates (2022); Sumayya Vally, Counterspace (2021); Junya Ishigami (2019) and Frida Escobedo (2018).

This year's selection was made by Serpentine CEO Bettina Korek, Artistic Director Hans Ulrich Obrist, Director of Construction and Special Projects Julie Burnell, Director of Curatorial Affairs and Public Practice Yesomi Umolu, Project Curator Alexa Chow and Curator at Large, Architecture and Site-specific Projects Natalia Grabowska, together with advisors Sou Fujimoto and David Glover. The intention is to choose architects who consistently extend the boundaries of contemporary architectural practice and to introduce these practitioners to wider audiences. Architects are asked to design a temporary structure that considers the historical, social and geographical context of the Serpentine. The Pavilion also functions as a meeting space and café by day and a place for learning, debate and entertainment at night.

Every year, the Pavilion plays host to the annual interdisciplinary live programme *Park Nights*. This year's programme features new commissions of music, poetry, performance and dance. Curated by Claude Adjil, *Park Nights 2024* reimagines what it means to come together, witness and share thought through live performance. The programme will take place on selected evenings throughout June to October and presents practitioners including Eun-Me Ahn, Anne Boyer, Don Mee Choi and Denise Riley.

This publication has been designed by the exceptional duo Choi Sung Min and Choi Sulki from Seoul-based design practice Sulki & Min and we thank them for their care and dedication in making this book. Conceived in close collaboration with Cho, the catalogue brings together contributors from across the world of architecture, art and poetry, all of whom inform Cho's architecture practice. Stefano Boeri recounts his encounter with Cho's Ring Dome, and writes about Cho's sensitivity towards the use of materials and approach in space-making. Kenneth Frampton, who taught Cho at the Graduate School of Architecture, Planning and Preservation (GSAPP) at Columbia University, traces Cho's practice, his roots, inspirations and development. Responding to the title *Archipelagic Void*, Alex Taek-Gwang Lee expands on the concept of the void and how it connects with Korean culture and history and the archipelagic thinking of Glissant. Beatrice Galilee brings forward Cho's multi-disciplinary practice in architecture, design and art, and how it provides fertile ground for Cho to design a Pavilion that brings these elements together. Award-winning poet Kim Hyesoon contributes a poem that explores the tactile experience of the Pavilion and its connection with our bodies. Artist Renée Green shares a series of handwritten notes, drawings and graphic diagrams, creating a unique space poem for this year's commission. Choreographer Eun-Me Ahn presents a collage of dancing bodies and architectural structures, playfully comparing the versatility of Cho's Pavilion to that of a Swiss Army knife. We are indebted to all contributors for sharing their knowledge, creativity and offering this multitude of perspectives.

Alongside the brilliant contributions, the catalogue also includes a series of images and drawings from Cho and Mass Studies to showcase the design process of the Pavilion. A photo essay by Iwan Baan captures the various ways in which visitors engage with the five 'islands' and the technical details of each structure. The publication also includes an extensive interview between the architect and Hans Ulrich Obrist, which introduces Cho's practice and traces the research, development and ideas behind the Pavilion.

First and foremost, we would like to offer our heartfelt thanks to Minsuk Cho for his energy, dedication and outstanding commitment to the Pavilion project and its related programming. His thorough research into the history of the Pavilion commission and topography of the site brings about an innovative design that uncovers new ways of interpreting the architectural centre, thereby creating a multifaceted Pavilion for visitors of all ages to come together. We would also like to acknowledge his team: Kisu Park, Junkoo Kang, Bumhyun Chun, Betty Kim, Minho Hong, Shinhyuk Kim, Younjae Choi, Jae Sok Surh, Yeonsu Hong, Seunghyun Ko, Seungmin Chung, Goya Yoon and Byungsoon Park (Thekujo) for their tireless dedication in realising this Pavilion.

We thank musician and composer Jang Young-Gyu for contributing such a captivating sound installation. It is a truly unique work that depicts the transition of the seasons through Korean vocal music and traditional instruments. Thanks also go to artist Heman Chong and archivist Renée Staal for letting us host *The Library of Unread Books* in the Pavilion. It was a joy to see visitors engaging and contributing to its growing collection by donating their own unread books to form a pool of common knowledge for the community.

We are hugely grateful to Goldman Sachs, the headline sponsor of the Serpentine Pavilion 2024, which is supporting this annual commission for the tenth consecutive year. Richard Gnodde and the team at Goldman Sachs are invaluable in realising this collaboration with us, and we thank them wholeheartedly.

Serpentine is truly indebted to the Samsung Foundation of Culture, Yongsoo Huh and the Korea Foundation for their invaluable support of the Pavilion 2024 commission. This programme could not be realised without their crucial contributions.

Our sincerest thanks also extend to Sou Fujimoto, who served as advisor on the selection committee for generously sharing his invaluable knowledge and time with us. We would also like to thank David Glover, our longstanding technical consultant, who worked closely with Cho and the wider Pavilion team. His expertise and advice are essential to the success of this commission.

We thank our Technical Advisors, AECOM led by Jon Leach and his team: Louise McGinley, Ben Lewis, James Wright, Sara Mandoki, Hope Francis, Dan Wallington, Madi Taylor, Davide Solari, Arianna Foltran, Issac Refalo, Iain Heath, Elizabeth Green, Tarun Perry, Roddy Prayag, Natalie Harris and Stuart East. Their continued expertise is fundamental to the realisation of the commission. We are very grateful to Stage One Creative Services Ltd, in particular Ted Featonby, Tim Leigh and Alan Doyle, who work closely with the architects and the Serpentine each year to construct the Pavilion.

This year's commission would not have been possible without the support of our Gold Sponsor: Weil; Silver Sponsor: Gallowglass Health and Safety, in particular Steve Kearney; Neil Raithatha at Zumtobel and THORN; Bronze Sponsors: DP9, in particular Barnaby Collins and Theo Barker; Jeremy Singleton at The Technical Department. Further advisors whom we would like to acknowledge are Andrew Scattergood, Darren Share and Andrew Williams at the Royal Parks; Westminster City Council District Surveyor's Office, in particular Samir El Nagi and Garnet Gordon; David Doyle at the London Fire Brigade; and Friends of Hyde Park and Kensington Gardens. All of these organisations and individuals were instrumental throughout this project, and we are hugely grateful for their continued support.

We would like to offer our continued gratitude to Bloomberg Philanthropies, in particular our Chairman Michael R. Bloomberg, Patti Harris and Jemma Read, for partnering with us on Serpentine's Bloomberg Connects App, which enables us to extend the reach of our audiences.

The Serpentine Council is an extraordinary group of individuals who provide ongoing and important assistance to enable us to deliver our ambitious Art, Architecture, Civic, Ecologies, Education, Live and Technology Programmes. We are also sincerely appreciative of the support from the Corporate Members, Americas Foundation, Patrons and Future Contemporaries of Serpentine.

Finally, we would like to express our thanks to the Serpentine team who made this Pavilion possible, in particular Julie Burnell, Director of Construction and Special Projects, who has overseen seventeen Pavilions to date. Her continued energy and unwavering commitment to the project are essential. We also thank Yesomi Umolu, Director of Curatorial Affairs and Public Practice, and Alexa Chow, Project Curator, who with the support of Natalia Grabowska, Curatorial Advisor, worked closely with Minsuk Cho, the design team and the wider Serpentine team to see this project come to fruition. Further thanks are due to Gonzalo Herrero Delicado, Project Curator, who, together with Cho and the curators of this year's commission realised the sound installation and *The Library of Unread Books*.

Hans Ulrich Obrist, Artistic Director
Bettina Korek, Chief Executive

Hans Ulrich Obrist is Artistic Director of Serpentine in London, and Senior Advisor at LUMA Arles. Prior to this, he was the Curator of the Musée d'Art Moderne de la Ville de Paris. Since his first show 'World Soup' (The Kitchen Show) in 1991, he has curated more than 350 exhibitions. Obrist's recent publications include *Ways of Curating* (2015), *The Age of Earthquakes* (2015), *Lives of the Artists, Lives of Architects* (2015), *The Extreme Self: Age of You* (2021), *140 Ideas for Planet Earth* (2021), *Edouard Glissant: Archipelago* (2021), *James Lovelock: Ever Gaia* (2023), *Remember to Dream* (2023) and *Une vie in Progress* (2023).

Bettina Korek is the Chief Executive of Serpentine, an arts institution in London's Kensington Gardens that has pioneered innovation and collaboration in contemporary art, architecture and more since 1970. She has two decades of experience as an arts leader in her hometown of Los Angeles, where she most recently was the Executive Director of Frieze Los Angeles.

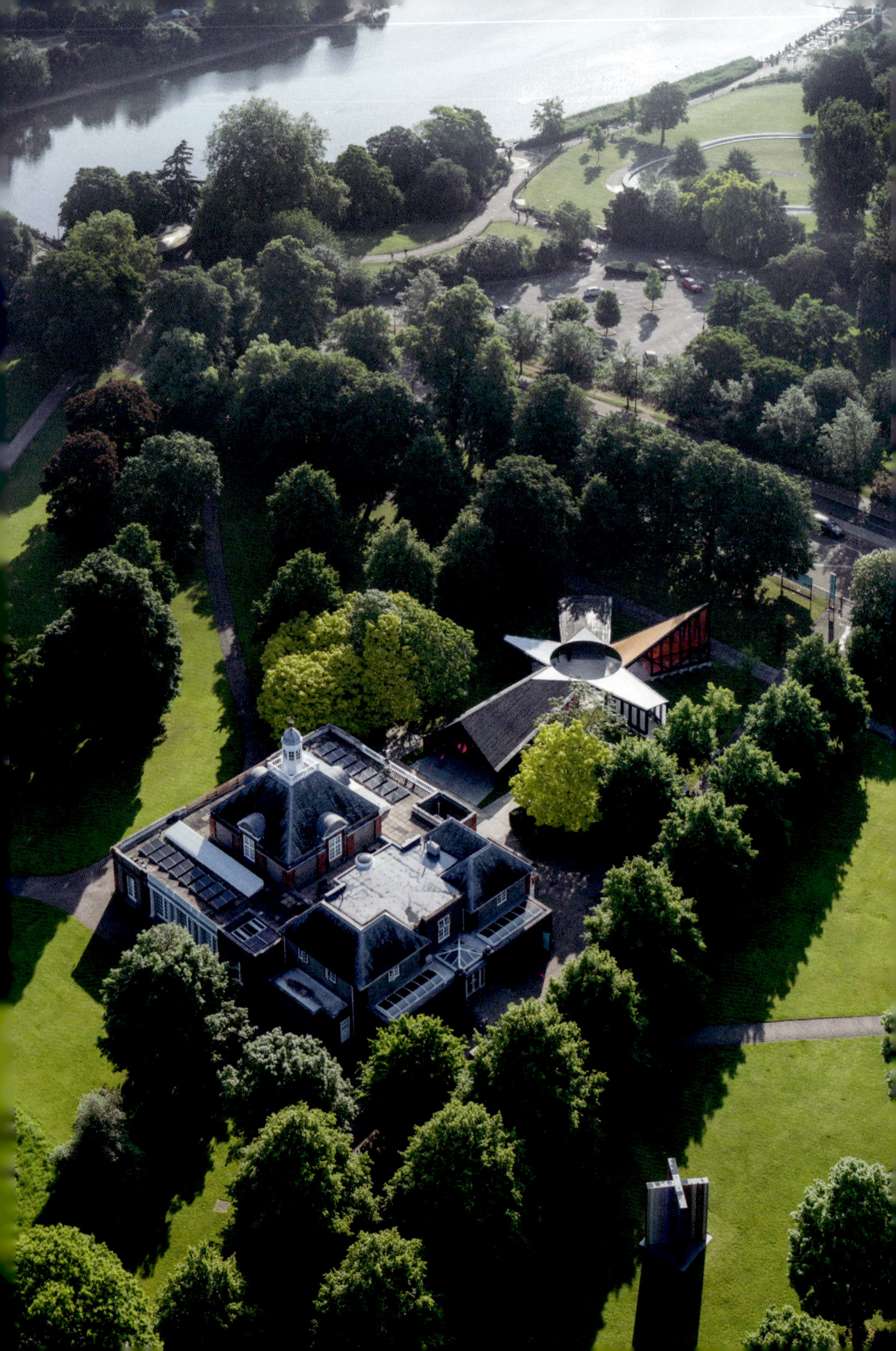

Sponsor's Foreword

We are immensely proud to have collaborated with Serpentine for ten consecutive years on the iconic architectural Pavilion commission. Over this period, the project has attracted a diverse group of architects who have showcased their talents and shared their unique global perspectives.

This year, we are looking forward to celebrating Minsuk Cho and his firm Mass Studies. Cho's design is entirely unique and promises to be a vibrant and fascinating space for us all to enjoy. We congratulate Mass Studies on their first official structure in the UK and extend our warm welcome to our capital.

London remains an important cultural centre. Arts and culture are in our DNA and ambitiously creative projects like the Serpentine Pavilion continue to engage Londoners and attract millions of visitors to our great city.

We extend our sincere gratitude to the Serpentine team for their steadfast commitment to showcasing original ideas in art and architecture, and to all of our partners on the Pavilion project who collectively continue to make it a reality.

Richard Gnodde,
CEO, Goldman Sachs International

Aerial view of the Serpentine Pavilion 2024.
Photo by Iwan Baan

Richard J Gnodde is chief executive officer of Goldman Sachs International. His leadership responsibilities cover all of the firm's businesses outside of North America. He has been a member of the Management Committee since 2003 and also serves on the Firmwide Reputational Risk Committee and chairs the European Management Committee. He serves as a Trustee of the University of Cape Town Trust and The Foundation and Friends of the Royal Botanic Gardens, Kew. He also serves on the Campaign Board of Cambridge University and is a member of the Alzheimer's Research UK Pioneers' Circle.

Serpentine Pavilions 2000–2023

Serpentine Pavilion 2000, Zaha Hadid

Serpentine Pavilion 2001, Daniel Libeskind with Arup

Serpentine Pavilion 2002, Toyo Ito with Arup

Serpentine Pavilion 2003, Oscar Niemeyer

Serpentine Pavilion 2004 (unrealised), MVRDV with Arup

Serpentine Pavilion 2005, Álvaro Siza and Eduardo Souto de Moura with Cecil Balmond, Arup

Serpentine Pavilion 2006, Rem Koolhaas with Cecil Balmond, Arup

Serpentine Pavilion 2007, Olafur Eliasson and Kjetil Thorsen

Serpentine Pavilion 2008, Frank Gehry

Serpentine Pavilion 2009, Kazuyo Sejima and Ryue Nishizawa, SANAA

Serpentine Pavilion 2010, Jean Nouvel

Serpentine Pavilion 2011, Peter Zumthor

Serpentine Pavilion 2012, Herzog & de Meuron and Ai Weiwei

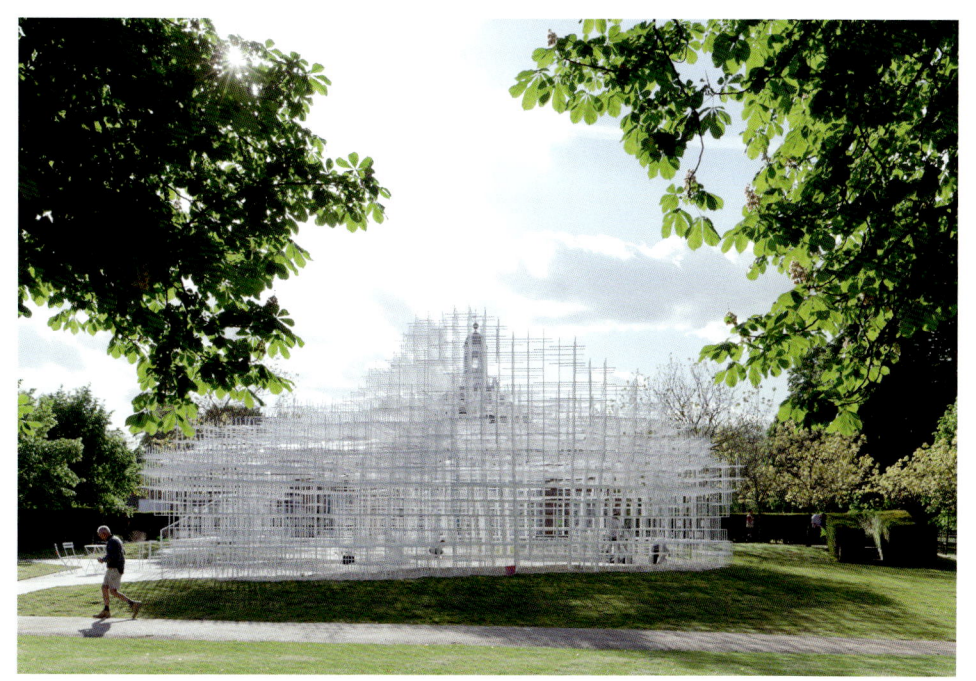

Serpentine Pavilion 2013, Sou Fujimoto

Serpentine Pavilion 2014, Smiljan Radić

Serpentine Pavilion 2015, Selgascano

Serpentine Pavilion 2016, BIG — Bjarke Ingels Group

Serpentine Pavilion 2017, Kéré Architecture

Serpentine Pavilion 2018, Frida Escobedo

Serpentine Pavilion 2019, Junya Ishigami + Associates

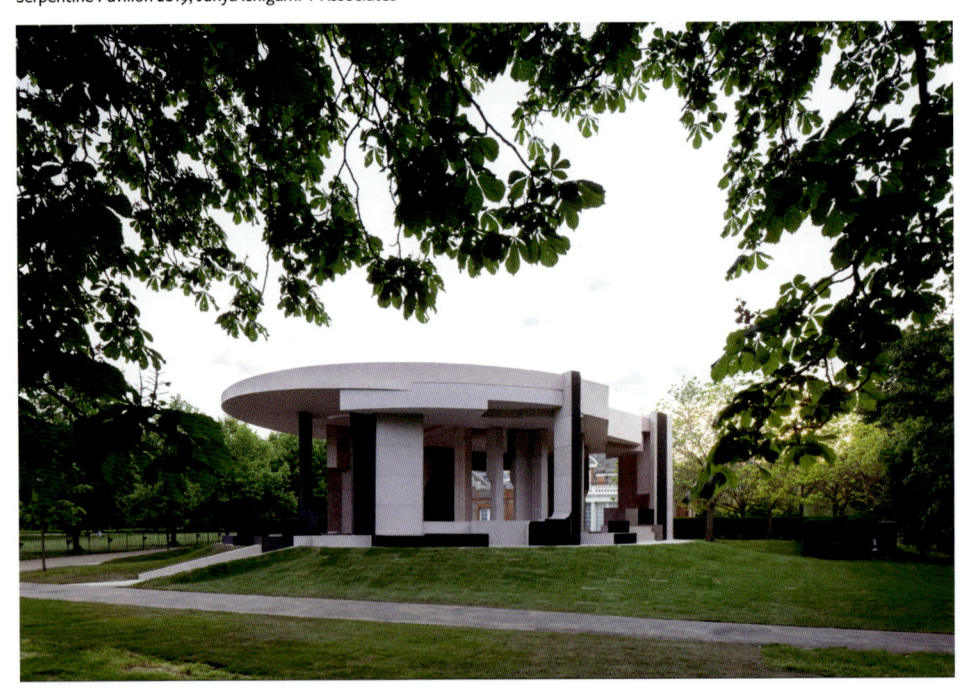

Serpentine Pavilion 2021, Sumayya Vally, Counterspace

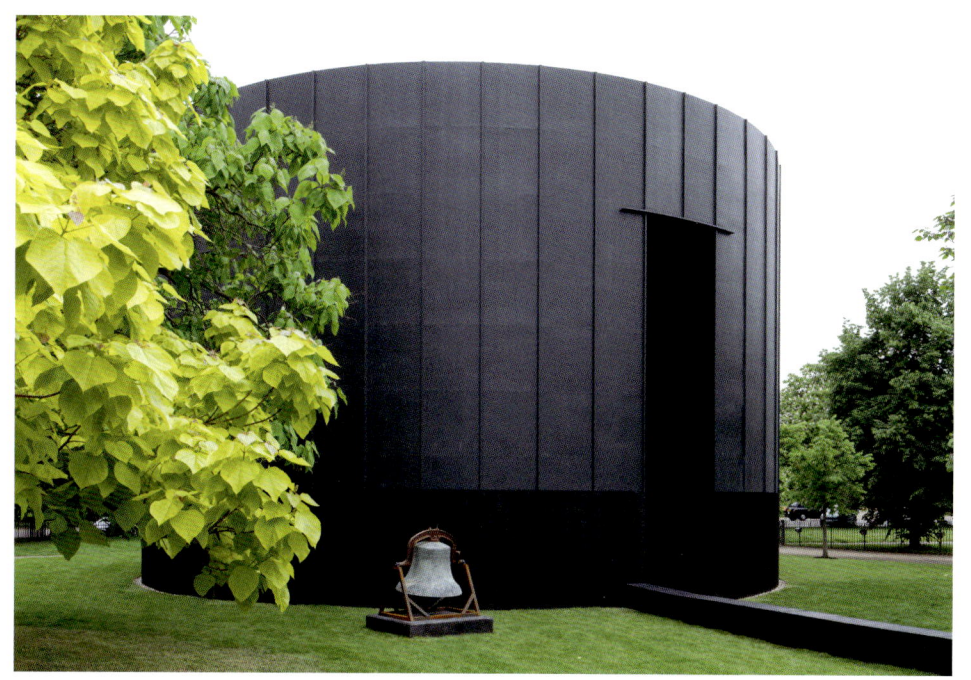

Serpentine Pavilion 2022 *Black Chapel*, Theaster Gates, with architectural support by Adjaye Associates

Serpentine Pavilion 2023 *À table*, Lina Ghotmeh — Architecture

Thank You

Trustees of Serpentine
Michael R. Bloomberg, *Chairman*
The Hon Felicity Waley-Cohen CBE and Barry Townsley CBE, *Co-Vice Chairmen*
Marcus Boyle, *Treasurery*
Andrew Cohen
Nicoletta Fiorucci Russo Off. OSI
Lady Elena Foster
Maja Hoffmann
Ruth Mackenzie CBE
Megha Mittal
Robert Rosenkranz
Amanda Sharp OBE
Jonathan Wood
Lynette Yiadom-Boakye

Council of Serpentine
Lady Elena Foster, *Chair*
Narmina Marandi and Francis Sultana, *Co-Heads of Cultural and Social Affairs Committee*
The Hon Felicity Waley-Cohen CBE, *Head of Education Committee*
Iwan Wirth, *Head of Exhibitions Committee*
Nina Fialkow and Kristín Ólafsdóttir, *Co-Heads of Film Committee*
Saffron Aldridge
Robin and Esha Arora
Veronica and Lars Bane Foundation
Ms Goga Ashkenazi
Sofia Barattieri-Weinstein and Brian Weinstein
Erin Bell and Michael Cohen
Nicolas Berggruen
Mrs Laurence Bet-Mansour
Blavatnik Family Foundation
Ivor Braka
Donatella Campioni
Kate and John Carrafiell
Tom and Ruth Chapman
Priscilla and Louis de Charbonnieres
XiaoMeng Cheng

Nick and Caroline Clarry
Andrew Cohen
Irene and John Danilovich
Alexander DiPersia
Griet Dupont
Carla du Manoir
Alia El Gazzar
James and Jennifer Esposito
Dr Paul Ettlinger, Raimund Berthold and The London General Practice
Mr Fares Fares and Mrs Tania Fares
Idit and Moti Ferder
Nina and David Fialkow
Nicoletta Fiorucci Russo and Giovanni Russo
Ms Silvia Fiorucci
Candia Fisher
The Lord and Lady Foster of Thames Bank
Futura Seoul — Dahoe Ku
Alys and Jim Garman
Sasan and Yassmin Ghandehari
Good Produce Ltd.
Richard and Odile Grogan
Mr Huh Yongsoo
Sue Hostetler-Wrigley
Alex Ionescu
Frédéric Jousset
Kirsh Foundation
Nicolette Kwok
Murtaza and Manal Lakhani
Xin Li-Cohen
Camilla and John Lindfors
Mrs Aarti Lohia
Sanda Lwin and Farhad Karim
Narmina and Javad Marandi
Samantha McManus
Usha and Lakshmi N. Mittal
Alexandre and Mahsa Mouradian
Anh Nguyen and Christopher Schläffer
Batia and Idan Ofer
Kristín Ólafsdóttir and Thor Björgólfsson
Julia and Hans Rausing
Christian Ravina and Robin Woodhead
Patrizia Re Rebaudengo
Frances Reynolds
Sybil Robson Orr and Matthew Orr
Bianca Roden
Galerie Thaddaeus Ropac, London · Paris · Salzburg
Mr and Mrs Spas Roussev
Karen and Ely Michel Ruimy
Almine Ruiz-Picasso

Suzan Sabancı Dinçer
Mr and Mrs Jean Salata
Dr Catherine Schmid
Anders and Yukiko Schroeder
Andrée Shore
Tatiana Silva
Thea Sprecher
Kate and John Storey
John Studzinski CBE
Odeta Stuikys
Francis Sultana and David Gill
Antigone Theodorou and Stefan Bollinger
Madeleine Thomson
Laura and Barry Townsley
Mrs Aizel Trudel
Piril and Igno Van Waesberghe
Tamara Varga
Robert and Felicity Waley-Cohen CBE
White Cube Limited
Millicent Wilner
The Lars Windhorst Foundation
Manuela and Iwan Wirth
Jonathan and Lucy Wood
Poju Zabludowicz and Anita Zabludowicz OBE

Programmes supported by
180 Studios
1OF1 AG
Sarah Arison
Debbie and Glenn August
Veronica and Lars Bane
Hannah Barry
Deborah Beckmann Kotzubei and Jacob Kotzubei
Diego Berdakin
Bloomberg Philanthropies
Camalotte Foundation
Cockayne — Grants for the Arts
James Cohan Gallery
The John S Cohen Foundation
Cristea Roberts Gallery
Nancy and Steven Crown
Suzanne Deal Booth Cultural Trust
Don Quixote Foundation
Katherine Farley and Jerry Speyer
Nina and David Fialkow
Nicoletta Fiorucci Foundation
Ford Foundation
Stephen Friedman
Gagosian
Goodman Gallery
Kenneth C. Griffin
Agnes Gund
HENI
Hostetler/Wrigley Foundation
Yongsoo Huh

Kadima Foundation
The Korea Foundation
The London Community Foundation
Luma Foundation
The Marandi Foundation
Mayor of London
Maria Lassnig Foundation
Victoria Miro
Aditya and Megha Mittal
Jarl Mohn
Angella Nazarian
Gilberto Pozzi
Ressler-Gertz Family Foundation
Frances Reynolds
Sybil Robson Orr and Matthew Orr
Thaddaeus Ropac
The Rosenkranz Foundation
Suzan Sabancı
Jordan Schnitzer, The Harold & Arlene Schnitzer CARE Foundation
Jessica Silverman, San Fransico
Reggie and Leigh Smith
Sprüth Magers
The Julia Stoschek Collection
Adam and Jessica Sweidan
Terra Foundation for American Art
Rolly van Rappard
Oliva Walton and The Momentary
White Cube
Lars Windhorst
David Zwirner

Capital Gifts
Wolfson Foundation

Platinum Corporate Benefactors
AECOM
Bloomberg
Dior
Dorsia
Goldman Sachs
Lugano Diamonds
Muse, The Rolls-Royce Art Programme
Tezos Ecosystem
VIVE Arts
Weil, Gotshal & Manges

Gold Corporate Benefactors
Google
Hublot
Ruinart Maison
Northern Trust

Silver Corporate Benefactors
Edwardian Hotels London
Gallowglass Health and Safety
The Pictet Group

Bronze Corporate Benefactors
DP9
Stage One
The Technical Department
Whispering Angel
Zumtobel

Principal Corporate Members
Bloomberg
Citi
Foster + Partners

Annual Corporate Members
Julius Baer

Associate Corporate Members
CBRE
London Essence
The Peninsula Hotels
Travers Smith

Serpentine Americas Foundation Board
Susan Danilow, *Board Chair*
Marina Abramović
Sarah Arison
Debbie August
Abigail Baratta
Kasseem, Swizz Beatz, Dean, *Honorary Member*
KAWS
Bettina Korek, *ex officio*
Robin Saunders
Rirkrit Tiravanija
Ted Vassilev

Serpentine Americas Foundation Supporters
Sarah Arison | Arison Arts Foundation
Debbie and Glenn August
Abby and Matt Bangser
Abigail Baratta
Diego Berdakin
Berggruen Charities
Blavatnik Family Foundation
Deborah Beckmann and Jacob Kotzubei
Camalotte Foundation
Wendy and Matthew Cherwin
James Cohan Gallery
Nancy and Steven Crown
John and Irene Danilow
Susan and Greg Danilow

Suzanne Deal Booth Cultural Trust
Sarah de Blasio and The DeBlasio Family Foundation
The Dinan Family Foundation
Alexander DiPersia
Jennie and Richard DeScherer, *In Memoriam*
Jamie Drake
Carla and Gerald Du Manoir
James and Jennifer Esposito Shaari Ergas
Katherine Farley and Jerry Speyer
Lisa S. Firestone
Fuhrman Family Foundation
Katia Francesconi Charitable Fund
Lauren Schor Geller and Martin Geller
Claire Hofmann and Ben Goldhirsh
Laurie and Peter Grauer
Scott D. Greenberg
Kenneth C. Griffin
Agnes Gund
Mimi Haas
Josh Harris and Layla Nemazee
Marlene Hess and James Zirin
Hostetler/Wrigley Foundation
Alex Ionescu
Thomas L. Kempner Jr. Foundation Inc.
Elizabeth Khuri and Otis Chandler
Nicole and Joel Klein
Eric Kranzler
Marie-Josée and Henry Kravis
Nancy Lainer
Vincent LaPadula
Agnes Lew
Xin Li-Cohen
Elizabeth S. and J. Jeffry Louis
Marian Goodman Foundation
Samantha McManus
Lachlan Miles and Christopher Hill
Pamela and Jarl Mohn
The Moore Charitable Foundation
Sandra Muss
Angella Nazarian
Patty Newburger and Brad Wechsler
Scott Rechler | Rechler Philanthropy, LLC
Ressler-Gertz Family Foundation
Sybil Robson Orr and Matthew Orr

The Rosenkranz Foundation
Steve and Kaayla Roth Foundation
A.S.C. Rower
Doug Schoen
Jordan Schnitzer, The Harold & Arlene Schnitzer CARE Foundation
Carla Shen
Tatiana Silva
Samira Sine
Ed Skyler | Citi
Reggie and Leigh Smith
Tishman Speyer
Wendy Stark Morrisey
Gillian and Robert Steel
Kate and John Storey
Odeta Stuikys Rose
Grazka Taylor
Roxann Taylor
Piril and Igno Van Waesberghe
Simona and Ted Vassilev
Oliva Walton and The Momentary
Hope Warschaw
Maureen White and Steven Rattner
Bonnie and Darrin Woo
Barbara and David Zalaznick

Patrons
Kate Gordon, *Chair*
Joy Adams
Alka and Ravin Agrawal
Nora Alangari
Almine Rech
Jose Antonio Alcantara
Yassaman Ali
Kamel Alzarka
Zachery and Deanne Anderson
Nur Avas
Parita Bagheri
Dr Bettina Bahlsen
Caroline Boseley
Romanos Elie Brihi
Mr Adam Brunk and Dr Madeleine Haddon
Burger Collection, Hong Kong
Chantal and Greg Chamandy
Radhika Chanana
Katherine Chapman Stemberg
Quaid Childers
Greg and Ania Coffey
Niki Cole
COLERIDGE CAPITAL
Pilar Corrias
Frederic Court
Thomas Croft
Yoav Dangoor
Colleen De Bonis

Sophie Diedrichs
Valentina Drouin
Genevieve Dunn
Maryam Eisler
Leonie Fallstrom
Alessandro Maria Ferreri
Kateryna Filippi
Mr Tim Flynn
Katia Francesconi
Mala Gaonkar
Amy Gardner
Houda Ghazal
Richard Grosse
Francesca Guagnini
Oliver Haarmann
Linford Haggie
Maxine Hargreaves-Adams
Josh and Layla Harris
Isabelle Henkell von Ribbentrop
Sanjay and Anu Hinduja
Kelly Hoppen
Joanna Iglauer
Eva and Iraj Ispahani
Mrs Mary Jeffers
Mr Vladimir Kantor
Charles Karsten
Guldeep Kohli
Vivian Landau Wipf
Maged Latif
Lyndon and Sophie Lea
Simon and Lily Liebel
Daniel Macmillian
Cary Martin and Adrienn Almásy-Martin
Alexandra McManus
Pramod Mittal
Natalia Miyar
Manuela Morgano
John Mortimer
Maiguelle Moulene
Natasha Müller
Richard Muirhead
Opera Gallery London
Asli Ozok
Maureen Paley
Asta Paulauskaite
Alexander Platon
Ahmed Rahman
Marc Renard-Payen
Luciana Rique
Kimberley Robson
Francesca Roni
Tarika Sawhney
Ajazul Shah
Henrietta Shields
Nayrouz Tatanaki
Michael Tian and Sharon Zhu
Adi Tiroche
Ms Warly Tomei
Emily Tsingou

Anastasia Velikovsky
Andrianna Whish
Ashley White
Julia Zaouk
Mr and Mrs Zorbibe
David Zwirner

Future Contemporaries Committee
Robert Sheffield and
  Nicholas Kirkwood,
  Co-*Chairs*
HRH Princess Eugenie of York
Alayo Akinkugbe
Alia Al-Senussi
Milo Astaire
Ashkan Baghestani
Hannah Barry
Evelyn Booth-Clibborn
Efe Cakarel
Chiara Carboni
Laura De Gunzburg
Alex Eagle
The Hon Paola Foster
Jasper Greig
Anna Guggenbuehl Landau
Joe Kennedy
Karen Levy
Joanna Masiyiwa
Alexander Hankin
Eugenio Re Rebaudengo
Annabelle Scholar
Hikari Yokoyama

Future Contemporaries Members
Jade Adams
Toluwani Adejuyigbe
Chard Adio
Jose Antonio Alcantara
Sara AlRashed
Aurore Ankarcrona Hennessey
Gianluca Arrigoni
Mila Askarova
Marco Assetto
Mrs. Bahamdan
Tosca Baharani
Josephine May Bailey
Adam Baldwin
Alastair Balfour
Mrs Natasha Barnaba
Isabel Barrachina Gomez
Anna Nora Berstein
Valeria Biamonti
Maribelle Bierens
Sabina Bilenko
Lucas Bitencourt
Berry Bloomingdale
Julia Bolgova
Cassandra Bowes
Monelle Bradshaw

Leonie and Mikael Brantberg
Keeli Brantl
Romanos Elie Brihi
Žanete Bukarte
Alexandra Burston
Jonny Burt
Manfredi Campioni de Filippo
Alaric Cao
Jez Cartwright
Louis Chapple
Tahira Chawla
Cherry Cheng
Claudia Cheng
Chen Chowers
Nathan Clements-Gillespie
William Comfort
Ilayda Danisman
Filipe de Almeida Assis
Sophie De Mello Franco
Sophie Dickson
Margarita Domuschieva
Catherine Doronin
Carolina Drago
Warren Ehgoetz
Izly El-Hammouti
Angela Enzo
Rayan Fayez
Eduardo Foster
Phoebe Forster
Natalia Fuller, Galerie
  Max Hetzler
Maria Garmaeva
Yasmin Gee
Mikel Giordano
Adam Gordon
Martell Graf Von Hardenberg
Taymour Grahne
Nico Guardansai
Lydia Guett
Bibi Hamidi
Celina Hares
Laura M. Herman
S Holt
Amanda Ibrahim
Adam Irving
Domino Jahn Vegetti
Charles Janeway
Millie Jason Foster
Javier Jileta
Peter Jones
Nicole Kaiser
Fereniki Kalamida
Zoe Karafylakis Sperling
Simmy Kaur
Shakil Karim
Minnie Kemp
Bella Kesoyan
Victoria Kleiner
Cordelia Knaack
Mrs Sonja Koenig
Casey Kohlberg

Yulia Kondakova
Mimi Koné
Dustin Kronsbein
Darya Kravchenko
Anna Kuchina
Cansu Kucuk
Philip Kwok
Flavia Lascetti
Arianna Laufer
Dominic Sylvia Lauren
Charles Le Pelley du Manoir
Pinyuan Li
Sam Lincoln
Matilda Liu
M-C Llamas
Simon Lyall-Cottle
Sonia Mak
Jean-David Malat
  JD Malat Gallery
Florence B M Mather
Magnus and Maria-Theresia
  Mathisen
Lena McCroary
Jayne Mckenna
Alexandra Meyers
Olivia Mieke-Maria Paulina
  Martha
Abigail Miller
Nina Moaddel
Francisco Mourao
Mu Qing
Kate Munk
Kevin Nathan
Devon Nocera
Charlotte Rohani
  Eliza Osborne
Charlie Pannell
Pietro Pantalani
Aurore Pasquet
Santa Pastare
Dyvia Pathak
Jan-Christoph Peters
Sophie Philippe
Ryan Poon
Polina Proshkina
Mr and Mrs Alexander
  Purcell Rodrigues
Jacob Rawel
Brooke Reese
Ariana Regalado
Piotr Rejmer
Jonathan Ridgway
Sophia Robert
Niklas Röhling
Anastasia Ruimy
Natasha Ryumina
Phoebe Saatchi Yates
Ceyda Sabancı Dinçer
Haluk Sabancı Dinçer
Valerie Sadoun
Kiara Salazar

Salima Sarsenova
Sally Eugenia Schwartz
Kitty Shenlin Mai
Miss Alaira Tirtha Shetty
Bianca Shi
Wei Shi
Skylar Xie
Oksana Smirnova
Nicolas Sorbac
Joseph Spieczny
Mithra Stevens
Stephanie Stevens
Kira Streletzki
Jana Suhani Soin
Gigi Surel
Roxana Sursock Karam
Molly Susman
Ying-Hsuan Tai
Aizhan Tampayeva
Leopold Thun
Philip Tomei
Milan Tomic
Margo Trushina
Elina Tsokri
Jason Tucker
Dexter Ukaegbu
Alina Uspenskaya
Rachel Verghis
Angelina Volk
Matilda Liu
Alexa and Marcus
  Waley-Cohen
Georgina Walker
Luning Wang
Pamela Weinstock
Tish Weinstock
Katy Wickremesinghe
Agata Woloszczuk
Susan Wu
Yuyao Xie
Dr Penny Dan Xu
Arthur Yates
Maya and Roy Zabludowicz
Nabil El Zaouk
Fabrizio D. Zappaterra

And any Council, Patrons,
Serpentine America
Supporters, and Future
Contemporaries who wish to
remain anonymous

And kind assistance from
The Royal Parks

Bloomberg Philanthropies

Public Funding by
Arts Council England

Project Team

Pavilion Architect
Mass Studies

Principal Architect & Designer
Minsuk Cho

Team
Kisu Park
Junkoo Kang
Bumhyun Chun
Betty Kim
Minho Hong
Shinhyuk Kim
Younjae Choi
Jae Sok Surh
Yeonsu Hong
Seunghyun Ko
Seungmin Chung
Goya Yoon
Byungsoon Park (Thekujo)

Project Directors
Hans Ulrich Obrist,
   Artistic Director
Bettina Korek,
   CEO

Project Leader
Julie Burnell,
   Director of Construction and Special Projects

Curators
Yesomi Umolu,
   Director of Curatorial Affairs and Public Practice
Alexa Chow,
   Project Curator
Natalia Grabowska,
   Curatorial Advisor

Sound Commission and Library
Yesomi Umolu,
   Director of Curatorial Affairs and Public Practice
Claude Adjil,
   Curator at Large
Alexa Chow,
   Project Curator
Gonzalo Herrero Delicado,
   Project Curator

Engineering and Technical Design
Technical Consultant
David Glover

Technical Advisors
AECOM
   Jon Leach
   Louise McGinley
   Ben Lewis
   James Wright
   Sara Mandoki
   Hope Francis
   Dan Wallington
   Madi Taylor
   Davide Solari
   Arianna Foltran
   Issac Refalo
   Iain Heath
   Elizabeth Green
   Tarun Perry
   Roddy Prayag
   Natalie Harris
   Stuart East

Town Planning Consultants
DP9
   Barnaby Collins
   Theo Barker

Construction
Stage One Creative Services Ltd
   Ted Featonby
   Tim Leigh
   Alan Doyle
Gallowglass Health & Safety
   Steve Kearney
The Technical Department
   Jeremy Singleton

Project Advisors
Michael R Bloomberg,
   Chairman, Serpentine Board of Trustees
Sou Fujimoto,
   Architect
Andrew Scattergood,
   CEO, The Royal Parks
Darren Share,
   Director, The Royal Parks
Andrew Williams,
   Park Manager, The Royal Parks
Samir El Nagi,
   Senior Structural Engineer
Garnet Gordon,
   Senior Building Control Surveyor Westminster City Council
Issac Refalo,
   District Surveyor's Office (Building Control)
City of Westminster Planning
David Doyle,
   London Fire Brigade
Friends of Hyde Park and Kensington Gardens

This catalogue is published to accompany the Serpentine Pavilion 2024 *Archipelagic Void* designed by Minsuk Cho, Mass Studies, 7 June–27 October 2024

Serpentine Pavilion 2024
© Minsuk Cho, Mass Studies

Edited by Alexa Chow, Gonzalo Herrero Delicado and Yesomi Umolu
Copyedited by Melissa Larner
Translation from Korean by Emily Jungmin Yoon
Designed by Sulki & Min
Printed by Gomer Press in Wales, UK

First published in 2024 by Serpentine and Verlag der Buchhandlung Walther und Franz König, Köln

© 2024 Minsuk Cho, Mass Studies; Serpentine, London; the authors; and Verlag der Buchhandlung Walther und Franz König, Köln

All rights reserved. No part of this publication may be reproduced, stored in a retrieval system or transmitted in any form or by any means, electronic, mechanical, photocopying, recording or otherwise without prior permission of the publishers. The publishers of this book are committed to respecting the intellectual property rights of others. Every effort has been made to trace copyright holders and to obtain their permission for the use of copyright material. The publishers apologise for any errors or omissions in the above list and would be grateful if notified of any corrections that should be incorporated in future reprints or editions of this book.

Published by

SERPENTINE

Serpentine
Kensington Gardens
London W2 3XA
Telephone +44 (0) 207 402 6075
Fax +44 (0) 207 402 4103
www.serpentinegalleries.org

Verlag der Buchhandlung Walther und Franz Konig
Ehrenstr. 4
D-50672 Köln

Bibliographic information published by the Deutsche Nationalbibliothek. The Deutsche National-bibliothek lists this publication in the Deutsche Nationalbibliografie; detailed bibliographic data are available on the Internet at http://dnb.d-nb.de.

Distribution

Europe
Buchhandlung Walther König
Ehrenstr. 4
D-50672 Köln
Telephone +49 (0) 221 / 20 59 6 53
verlag@buchhandlung-walther-koenig.de

UK & Ireland
ART DATA
12 Bell Industrial Estate
50 Cunnington Street
London W4 5HB
United Kingdom
Telephone +44 (0)208 747 10 61
Fax +44 (0)208 742 23 19
orders@artdata.co.uk

Outside Europe
D.A.P. / Distributed Art Publishers, Inc.
75 Broad Street, Suite 630
USA – New York, NY 10004
Telephone +1 (0) 212 627 1999
orders@dapinc.com

ISBN 978-1-908617-86-6
Serpentine, London

ISBN 978-3-7533-0688-9
Verlag der Buchhandlung Walther und Franz König, Köln

Serpentine Pavilion 2024
Made Possible by

Goldman Sachs

Major Support

SAMSUNG FOUNDATION OF CULTURE

Yongsoo Huh

KOREA FOUNDATION 한국국제교류재단

Technical Advisor

AECOM

Gold Sponsor

Weil

Silver Sponsors

STAGE ONE

GALLOWGLASS Health & Safety

THORN

ZUMTOBEL

Bronze Sponsors

DP9

the technical department

Technical Consultant

David Glover

Serpentine Supported by

Bloomberg Philanthropies

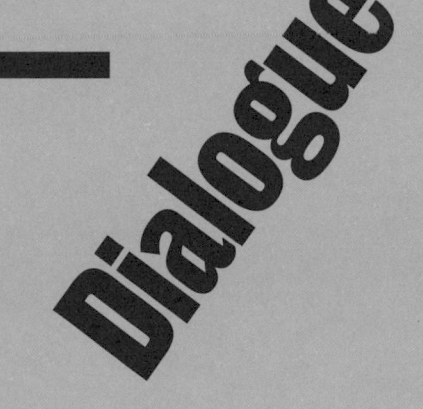

Serpentine Pavilion 2024
Archipelagic Void
Mass Studies

Dialogue

Serpentine Pavilion 2024 Archipelagic Void   Mass Studies

Edited by
Alexa Chow, Gonzalo Herrero Delicado
and Yesomi Umolu

Dialogue

Architect's Statement   2

Hans Ulrich Obrist in Conversation
with Minsuk Cho   4

Architect's Statement

The *Archipelagic Void* consists of five structures or 'islands' around an open space. Each segment of the Pavilion is unique in its shape and form, yet the same at the centre to create a circular void. Each part forms an arc at the centre top, one fifth of an eight-metre diameter circle, creating a space that balances between openness and enclosure.

The central void is reminiscent of a *madang*, a small courtyard in traditional Korean houses that can accommodate rich spatial narratives ranging from individual everyday activities to large collective rituals throughout the changing seasons.

The multifaceted Pavilion is envisioned as a 'content machine', each serving a purpose. The *Gallery* acts as the welcoming main entry, extending curatorial activities outside, with seasonal sound installations by musician and composer, Jang Young-Gyu. The *Auditorium* serves as a generous gathering area while to the north is an intimate *Library*, offering a moment of pause and hosting *The Library of Unread Books*, an artwork by artist Heman Chong and archivist Renée Staal. The *Tea House* honours the Serpentine South's early role as a tea pavilion. The *Play Tower*, the most open and exposed part, is equipped with a netscape to play, explore or rest.

Each component consists of two walls sitting on plinths that are used as covered or uncovered park benches and tables. Assembled, the parts become a montage of five distinct covered spaces and five open spaces of surrounding park in between, highlighted by varying natural light conditions.

The Serpentine Pavilion 2024 is simultaneously both contextual and abstract, site-specific and siteless. The structures mediate between the gently sloping topography of the Serpentine lawn and its surrounding elements.

The *Archipelagic Void* is both vernacular and modern. As in many places, traditional Korean buildings are built to be assembled and disassembled like a pavilion, supported by stone plinths. The primary material for this Pavilion is locally sourced limestone, Douglas fir timber and various colours and opacities of recyclable tensile membranes. The structure explores modern joinery techniques, allowing for effortless assembly and disassembly.

Minsuk Cho, April 2024

Minsuk Cho was born in Seoul and graduated from the Architectural Engineering Department of Yonsei University (Seoul, Korea) and the Graduate School of Architecture at Columbia University (New York, USA). After working in various firms, he returned to Korea in 2003 to open his own, Mass Studies. His work has received numerous awards including the Silver Award in the 'Pavilion Design' category for the Korea Pavilion at the World Expo 2010 Shanghai, accompanied by a Presidential Citation from the Korean government, and the Golden Lion Award for the Best National Pavilion while serving as the commissioner and co-curator of the Korean Pavilion at the 14th International Architecture Exhibition — la Biennale di Venezia, and the Hwagwan Medal Order of Cultural Merit from the Korean government.

Hans Ulrich Obrist
in Conversation with Minsuk Cho

Hans Ulrich Obrist: Let's begin at the beginning. Can you tell us how you came to architecture? Did you always want to be an architect as a child?

Minsuk Cho: In the late 60s, the population of Seoul was about four million people. It was already a fast-growing city but it was getting ready to explode even more. I have a vivid memory of that — the changing, very dynamic, embryonic condition of the city of Seoul, becoming the metropolis that it is now. I was born in an area that's not so far from where our office is located, in central Seoul, and as far back as I can remember, my childhood was in a construction site. That was my playground. I was quite a hyperactive kid, making things with all sorts of materials, from paper and clay to rocks and wood. This led me to aim for attending art school. My father is an architect, born in 1930, and soon to become ninety-five. He taught me that architecture isn't really a profession, but a way of life. He was very supportive of me wanting to be an artist and sent me to art classes during elementary school.

    Korea was a poor country compared to today's standards. There were some amazing buildings influenced by modernist architecture, but most of them were very pragmatic. At the time, architecture didn't really impress me. But one day, I saw my father had an architecture book with Le Corbusier's Ronchamp chapel on the cover. I asked him if that was also architecture, to which he replied, 'yes'. I was into artists like Picasso and Dalí, and slowly I shifted interests. I decided not to go to art school and instead went on to study architecture. That book was a turning point.

Hans Ulrich Obrist in conversation with Minsuk Cho at the Serpentine Pavilion 2024. Photo by Roland Halbe.

In your years of study, before you started your practice, which architects inspired you?

My obsession with Le Corbusier has always been very present. It started with my father, who worked for Kim Chung-up, who himself had worked for Le Corbusier in Paris in the mid-1950s. Also, through Kenneth Frampton, who was my teacher at Columbia University and a great influence to my career, I deepened my interest in Le Corbusier. During my graduate studies, I used the summer break to backpack around the world. I visited around twenty-eight buildings by Le Corbusier during that trip, including Chandigarh and many of his projects in Europe and Japan. This pilgrimage still goes on, and last year, I visited my thirty-third Le Corbusier building: Casa Curutchet in La Plata, Argentina. Rem Koolhaas has also been an important source of inspiration for me. His book *Delirious New York* was a great influence from very early on, since I was in my first year at university in the mid-80s.

One of Kenneth Frampton's seminal essays is 'Towards a Critical Regionalism: Six Points for an Architecture of Resistance' (1983), in which he advocates for a critical attitude towards the ongoing and globalised modernisation processes. To what extent did you feel, as a young architect in the 80s, that you had to negotiate the idea of globalisation presented in this essay?

In that sense, both Kenneth Frampton and Rem Koolhaas were both influential in different ways. Rem encouraged me to be curious and engage with that parallel universe opposite to the West where things happen in a canonical way. On the other hand, Kenneth was a very helpful guardian when I had to draw the line and decide whether I should take certain projects or not. Referencing Édouard Glissant's *Archipelagic Thinking*, they both created an archipelago of influences for me, where all the islands and the positions they represent can be understood as mountains connected below the water. Something I've realised more and more recently is that their influences, in some ways, came from seemingly opposite ends, but now, time has accumulated and also revealed that their rigour and ideas have validated each other.

I read in an interview that one of your favourite buildings is Lina Bo Bardi's Glass House in São Paulo. I find many connections with your work, in particular, between the Glass House and this year's Pavilion, both seamlessly blending the natural elements from the outside with the inside. Can you talk about the importance of Bo Bardi in your practice?

Eight years ago, I happened to visit Philip Johnson's Glass House in New York, and a few days later, to Lina Bo Bardi's Glass House — also known as Casa de Vidro. Despite the same name, the two buildings couldn't be more different. The Casa de Vidro is an amazing house that makes full use of the sloping hill on which it's situated. It's half suspended and half grounded at the same time. Unlike the better-known airy, suspended glass volume at the front, the back is a firmly grounded house with a traditional Spanish tile roof and even a pizza oven on the outside. Life really happens there and I was so surprised and moved by that. She was an overlooked figure for some time, often portrayed as a side note to the modernist 'canon', but she actually had her own unique vision. I think it comes from her approach of focusing a lot more on embracing life itself. The SESC Pompéia was also a revelation in the way she carefully dealt with the 'found' elements from its surroundings. It's a heroic, bold moment that shaped her vision, which I truly admire.

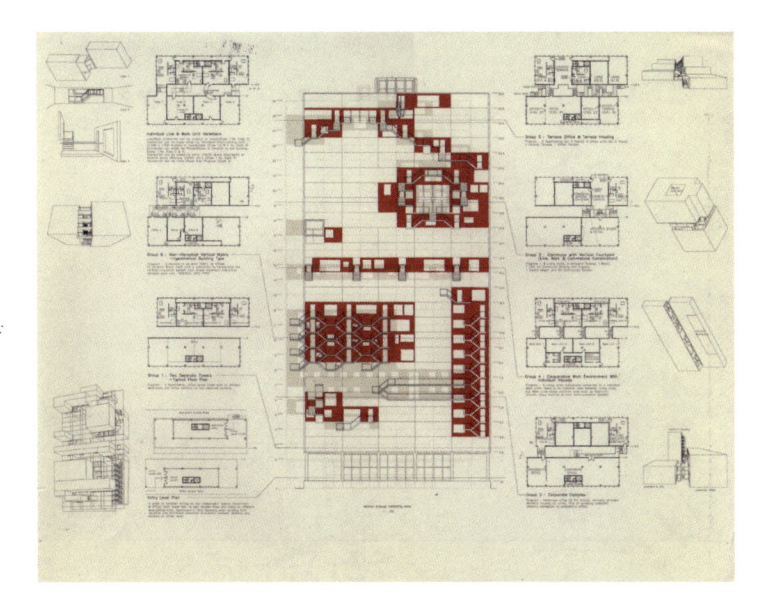

Minsuk Cho, *Siamese Towers: Reconfiguring Mies van der Rohe's 860 Lake Shore Drive Apartments* (Chicago, 1948–1951). First Prize, Shinkenchiku Residential Design Competition, 1994. © Minsuk Cho

Missing Matrix, 2008, in Seoul, South Korea. Photo by Kyungsub Shin

You opened your own office in 1998. What would you consider to be your number one entry in your catalogue raisonné?

I think if you include unbuilt works, then it goes back to 1994. It was a conceptual project for a competition organised by the Japanese magazine *Shinkenchiku*. Every year, they invite a prominent architect to come up with a theme related to residential issues. Fumihiko Maki, a big Japanese hero, proposed the theme 'Urban Dwelling', asking participants to consider the impact from new communication technologies such as the internet and redefine the relationship between our living and working conditions. I ended up being awarded the first prize with *Siamese Towers: Reconfiguring Mies van der Rohe's 860 Lake Shore Drive Apartment*. This became the starting point for our interrogation of high-rise buildings to improve social conditions in our practice.

And what's the number one in your catalogue raisonné in terms of built works?

Pixel House, 2003,
in Paju, South Korea.
Photo by Yong-Kwan Kim

It was a residential project that made me move back to Korea. At that time, I was still running a practice with James Slade. We started the project in 2001. It was a strange time in New York, just after 9/11, it was difficult to move beyond interior design commissions. However, in Korea, there is a place called Heyri Art Valley, a sort of utopian art community that was developed near the DMZ (demilitarised zone). We were approached by a family, a couple and their two children, seven and five years old. They were teachers who were blacklisted for a very long time because they had been student activists. They made their living through private tutoring and had recently been pardoned by the newly formed democratic government. At the time, and this is still going on, homogenous and repetitive apartment blocks were symptomatic of conformity. They wanted to have a fresh new start, with their children growing up in a different environment with unique memories, and so they chose an art community for their new home. They had a very small budget but made an ambitious demand, asking us to design a house that didn't look like anything that had ever existed in this world. The result was Pixel House, an eighty square metre house across two storeys.

How would you describe your methodology?

There are two words that are particularly important in my methodology: systematic and heterogeneity. When I came back to Korea, leaving behind Europe and New York, I realised architecture in the developed world was polarised between 'systematic' and 'heterogeneous' camps. The first is a brave group responsible for 95% of the buildings in the world. They often feel guilty because they're too busy to reflect or reassess the impact of their work. Then the second group is made up of a small group of sensitive architects who are often angry because they don't get to do much, although they are keenly aware of what's happening around them. Upon coming back to Korea, I decided to choose a different path — one that isn't defined by guilt or anger and can generate work that can be brave and sensitive at the same time, leaving behind that unrealistic overestimation or defeatist underestimation of what architecture can accomplish.

Both Cedric Price and Zaha Hadid understood pavilions as temporal spaces for experimentation, but pavilions also have a great potential to be truly public spaces. What role have pavilions played in your career?

I didn't realise until now that for the past twenty-one years, our practice has been continuously dealing with pavilions. We've built twelve pavilions so far, each very different, but all exploring how architecture can play a role in cultivating the public realm by bringing people together. Connecting to Cedric Price's reflection on the temporal condition of pavilions, each of our pavilions occupy a very particular space and moment in time. We've developed interesting 'time specific' ideas and methodologies to realise projects that sometimes only last for an hour, like the stages we designed for Eun-Me Ahn, or six months, as in the Korean Pavilion for the Shanghai Expo in 2010, or even much longer.

For us, pavilions have also been a great way to understand history. When we designed the Korean Pavilion in Shanghai, we looked at the larger context and the history of world expositions, which reflected the tumultuous process of modernity. We found moments like the Paris Exposition in 1900, in which the Korean Pavilion was a replica of one of the palace buildings in Seoul, showcasing the last Kingdom in Korea's history. It was a dignified building, yet feels out-of-place, a lone captive instead of doing what it's meant to do — being relational, creating a dialogue with its surroundings. Later, in the 1960s, after the Japanese colonial period, the pavilions re-emerged. They were built by early South Korean modernist pioneers such as Kim Chung-up, the architect of the South Korean Pavilion at the 1964 New York World's Fair and Kim Swoo Geun, who designed the Korean Pavilion for Expo '67, Montreal, then later, the Pavilion for Expo '70, Osaka, both presenting a much bolder, modernistic vision.

Korean Pavilion at the 1900 Paris Exposition, France

Korean Pavilion at the 2010 Expo, in Shanghai, China. Photo by Kyungsub Shin

For our pavilion in Shanghai, surrounded by bold objects — four circular pavilions, a somewhat absurd coincidence — we created an urban form instead, a hollowed-out box with nine different openings from all directions for people to enter and look inside, and vice versa.

You often collaborate with artists in your work. For the Korean Pavilion in the Shanghai Expo 2010, you collaborated with artists including Ik-Joong Kang. Can you talk about how you created this convergence?

The Shanghai Expo 2010 was a great success, with around 190 countries participating, including North Korea. Our pavilion received lots of attention probably because of its generosity. We knew many people would be waiting outside for long hours to go in to see the exhibition. So the hollowed-out box is like a waiting area, a space to be experienced somewhat similar to Bo Bardi's Museu de Arte de São Paulo (MASP).

When I was in New York, after Nam June Paik, Ik-Joong Kang was one of the best-known Korean artists in the 1990s. I didn't know him personally but I was

Korean Pavilion (interior view) at the 2010 Expo, in Shanghai, China.
Photo by Yong-Kwan Kim

moved by his works. During the proposal stage of the Korean Pavilion, his 10 x 10 cm 'unit paintings' came to my mind, and I decided to invite him to collaborate with us in the competition. He contributed 108 poems called *What I Know*, formed by unit paintings that were enlarged and digitally printed on panels integrated into the Pavilion. When the Pavilion was dismantled, Ik-Joong Kang signed and sold many of these panels and donated the money to a charity. It was a good demonstration for the afterlife of the Pavilion.

Pavilions are performative spaces and you've also designed stages. Please tell me more about your friendship with choreographer Eun-Me Ahn and how you connected and worked together.

My friendship with Eun-Me goes back to 1990, when I met her in Europe, during my three-month Le Corbusier pilgrimage, which I mentioned earlier. A couple of years later, Eun-Me moved to New York to study and we became very close allies. I performed many different roles for her at the humble beginning of her career in New York, when she self-produced her own shows. I started as a stage manager, doing all the work behind the stage, and I also did a couple of stage designs for her. We moved back to Seoul around the same time, and soon after that, when she directed the city festival in front of City Hall in 2008, she commissioned us to create a large suspended circular pavilion. We collaborated with Realities:United from Berlin, and created a large chandelier, fifty-five metres in diameter, called the May Palace, to host eight days of various performances for around six million people.

In her discipline of performing arts, the work reaches a climax towards the end. Architecture, however, begins with a climax — fantasising about the world we want to create — and then we spend years in the process of

Eun-Me Ahn, *Revolving Door*, 1999, New York. Stage deisgned by Minsuk Cho. Photo by Minsuk Cho; courtesy of Eun-Me Ahn

bringing those fantasies back down to the real world. These contrasting inversions have always fascinated me and made me envious of what she does, on top of the immediacy and fluidity that her discipline directly expresses and how it engages with very specific subjects.

Do you have any unrealised pavilions?

I don't know if you'd call it a pavilion, but it is an unrealised project that I'm very keen on. It's located in the DMZ. The DMZ is a very unique place, almost like a gift to humanity, because it's been untouched for more than seven decades since the war, with a flourishing ecosystem of more than 100 endangered species. This project, initiated by Choi Jae-Eun, an artist I deeply admire, invited contributions by artists and architects including Bijoy Jain, Lee Bul and Shigeru Ban, as well as scientists and environmentalists. Our contribution to the project repurposes one of the tunnels created by North Korea, which has now become a dark tourism destination. This hostile architecture for warfare is repurposed into a seed bank and an ecology library — a shared project for both Koreas and the rest of the world, to serve nature. Someday, I'd like to revisit this unrealised pavilion when the geopolitical circumstances allow — a situation that at the moment isn't very hopeful.

Bringing the two Koreas together was the focus for the South Korean Pavilion you curated for the Venice Architecture Biennale in 2014, which was awarded the Golden Lion. Can you talk a little bit more about this pavilion?

I'm glad you mentioned it because the DMZ project came just after that. Koolhaas's brief as director of the Biennale asked each national pavilion to look back 100 years and reflect on a period of 'absorbing modernity'.

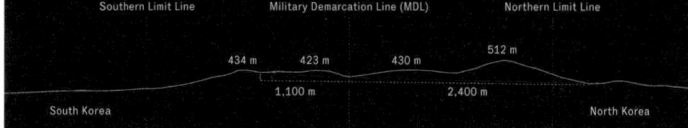

Site plan, *DMZ Vault of Life and Knowledge* (proposal), 2015, in Tunnel No. 2, DMZ, Korea. Image courtesy of Mass Studies

Sectional diagram, *DMZ Vault of Life and Knowledge* (proposal), 2015, in Tunnel No. 2, DMZ, Korea. Image courtesy of Mass Studies

When I made the proposal, I didn't know much about North Korea. However, it was obvious to me that if we only showcased South Korea, we'd be missing half of the story. A hundred years ago, Korea was one country, albeit under Japanese colonial rule. While researching the history of the Korean Pavilion in Giardini, we learned that the last opportunity to build a national pavilion there was granted thanks to Nam June Paik. After winning the Golden Lion while representing the reunified Germany in 1993, Paik pitched the idea of a Korean Pavilion for both South and North Korea to Massimo Cacciari, a philosopher who was the then Mayor of Venice. This is the reason why the pavilion signage at the entrance reads 'Korea' as opposed to 'Republic of Korea'. Beyond the name at the entrance, that proposal didn't succeed, because the founder of North Korea abruptly passed away, making the geopolitical situation very tense. I was happy to continue this attempt to make it my own way, although I didn't know about this history at the beginning.

Crow's Eye View: The Korean Peninsula, 2014, at the Venice Biennale Korean Pavilion in Giardini, Venice, Italy. Photo by Kyungsub Shin

Another experience you and I have shared, was of course the Ring Dome where I did several talks. Can you talk about that?

I always give credit to Joseph Grima for this project. In 2007, Joseph visited my office and he showed interest in a small 3D printed model for an unrealised pavilion sitting behind my desk. Maybe a week later, he sent me an email with a picture he took of the model, enlarged three times bigger and photoshopped to fit on the small park next to the Storefront for Art and Architecture, where he was then director. He asked us if we could build it for the twenty-fifth anniversary of Storefront. He gave us a budget that was three times smaller than the budget for the original project, and that's how the hula-hoop idea came about. It was a project in which the budget limitations worked to our benefit.

After that, in 2008, we created a new and improved version for Stefano Boeri and *Abitare* magazine in Milan. That iteration was followed by another two in Japan and years later, one in South Korea. The latter was part of an exhibition at Plateau, also formerly known as the Rodin Gallery, which was a sister gallery of the Leeum Samsung

Ring Dome Plateau, 2014, in Seoul, South Korea. Photo by Kyungsub Shin

Eun-Me Ahn performing at Ring Dome Plateau, February 2015, in Seoul, South Korea. Photo by Mass Studies

Museum of Art in Seoul. They invited Mass Studies to present a solo show there, which was a very big honour given that we were the first architects to be exhibiting there. They asked us to create the Ring Dome inside the grand vestibule of the gallery, called the 'glass pavilion', occupied by two Rodin sculptures. However, the Ring Dome was always meant to be in a public space. So we accepted under the condition that they move the ticket counter further inside, right before entering the galleries, providing free entrance to the 'glass pavilion', which was where we installed the Ring Dome, like a Trojan horse. We held free events there every Saturday, surrounded by the two Rodin sculptures — a total of thirteen times, with Eun-Me as the grand finale.

Now let's talk about London. It would be interesting to hear what went through your head when you got the invitation to design the Serpentine Pavilion 2024.

I was actually quite surprised and it's been an amazing journey. My first and only in-person experience of the Serpentine Pavilion was in 2005, which was designed by Álvaro Siza and Eduardo Souto de Moura. I remember it was a very rainy day, but as a big admirer of the two architects, I went to visit their pavilion. I was all by myself, nobody was there. It was only me and the architecture. I still vividly remember the strong scent of damp earth within the space. For me, that experience was a good reminder that architecture should be able to offer a full spectrum of experiences, from just a single person alone creating a dialogue with the space, to the exhilarating collective moments, which, for me, was how I experienced many of the other Serpentine Pavilions through various media.
    In the process of drafting the proposal, we looked back at the history of the Serpentine Pavilion since 2000 — all of the twenty-two built ones. We wanted our pavilion to be a very site-specific response, not only in a physical and spatial sense, but also in relation to the site's history. We wanted to contribute to and continue to be part of this larger, unique narrative that had been built before us.
    We looked at all the previous Serpentine Pavilion site plans and realised that the majority, two-thirds of them were geometric shapes, such as circular and rectangular shapes, and the remaining one-third were free forms.

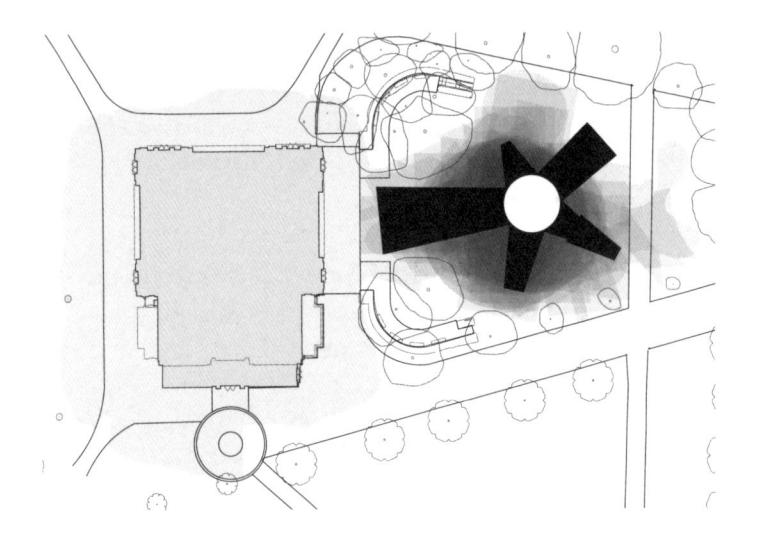

Overlap of the footprint of the Serpentine Pavilions (2000–2024) with void. Image courtesy of Mass Studies

Circular geometries were the most common. We also realised that six out of twelve built pavilions previously designed by Mass Studies, almost at the same period of the Serpentine Pavilions, were circular. We didn't think this was a coincidence, but that it might have to do with how the utopian idea of completeness and autonomy developed and evolved in the last century. Such twentieth-century examples can be seen from the Glass Pavilion by Bruno Taut for the 1914 Werkbund exhibition, the Dymaxion House by Buckminster Fuller in 1933 and even the designs for Drop City in Colorado in the 1960s and so on.

We thought these pavilions' complete and autonomous qualities also had a connection to follies in the English and French garden traditions, where the 'otherness' was brought in, whether through referencing architecture from another time, like the Roman ruins, or from other places, such as Chinese gazebos. In contrast, pavilions in my tradition have been about the 'here and now'; instead of inventing or bringing in new worlds, they are about discovering and highlighting their surroundings. I think it has to do with my culture, either Taoist or Buddhist, not believing in the afterlife, or heaven.

We thought it would complement the site's rich narrative to leave the most frequently used ground as a void and engage with the site's under-explored periphery as a balancing act. After we were appointed to design the Pavilion, I realised that previous projects, such as the Korean Pavilion for the 2010 Shanghai Expo or the more recent Won Buddhism Wonnam Temple, also addressed the multiplicity of the periphery, converging at a central open space to create connections and togetherness. These were the same ideas explored in different contexts.

You talked about the fact that you were never interested in the way architecture is consumed and produced in a single image, but in how the projects can reveal their context gradually. This happens with the Serpentine Pavilion, but also with the Won Buddhism Wonnam Temple. Can you tell us about this marvellous building?

As an agnostic, I hadn't accepted any other religious building commissions before this, but I felt that this was within my capacity. The Won Buddhist Temple, with around 250 members in its congregation, sought to replace its old concrete structure, which dates back to the 1960s. The project originated from a challenging and contradictory brief, emphasising both separation and connection. Old Buddhist temples were mostly situated in remote places, in the mountains. The journey to reach them is a kind of pilgrimage, an experience to purify yourself. But this temple is at the very centre of old Seoul, in a compressed urban situation where we had to create this journey. However, the cacophonous and bombastic urban development in and around the old city fabric created 'blockages', and dead ends, gradually disconnecting the temple from its surroundings and community. So our design process on one hand was an 'urban acupuncture'. The new temple is our response to the fast urbanisation that created disruptive conditions,

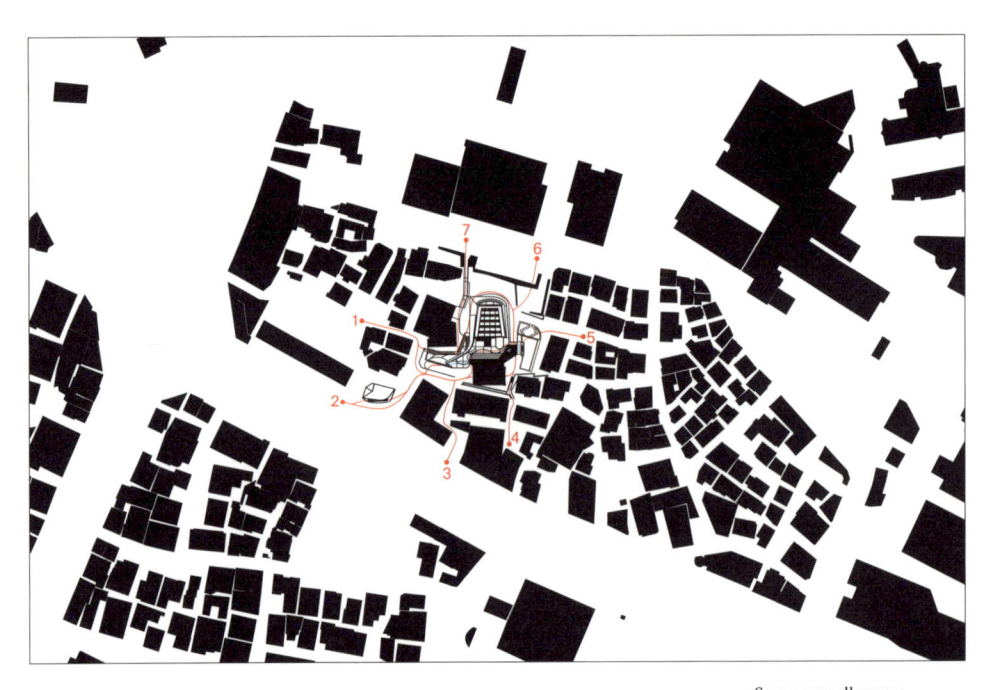

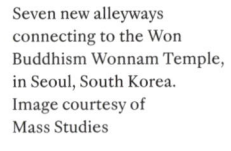

Seven new alleyways connecting to the Won Buddhism Wonnam Temple, in Seoul, South Korea. Image courtesy of Mass Studies

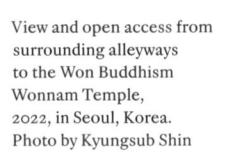

View and open access from surrounding alleyways to the Won Buddhism Wonnam Temple, 2022, in Seoul, Korea. Photo by Kyungsub Shin

20

particularly topographic and along the periphery of the temple complex. The result is a creature, some call it an octopus, with a quiet, secluded, central gathering space defining the 'spiritual environment'. It also rebuilds relationships and connections with its surroundings through seven legs or alleyways extending in all directions. This created an open environment suitable for this 'everyday religion', as they identify it, encouraging a balanced coexistence with the community's daily lives.

And then you came up with the idea of the *Archipelagic Void* which is connected to the idea of archipelagic thinking coined by Édouard Glissant. Can you talk about this connection and how this idea came about?

It was thanks to you that we named the Pavilion *Archipelagic Void*. It was a couple of days before we submitted our proposal that I found time and started reading your gift — a great little book, *The Archipelago Conversations* with Glissant. That's when I realised that what we were proposing was essentially an archipelago.

Despite being part of the vast Eurasian continent, South Korea has functioned as an archipelago for the past seventy-nine years, only reachable by plane or boat. This disruptive geographical isolation explains the multitude of architectural influences present in these very lands. I'm from a generation that grew up reading European philosophers like Derrida and Deleuze in my formative years. For many years, I immersed myself in the dialogue between philosophy and architecture that has evolved over the last 150 years, spanning across the Atlantic, between Europe and America, and with Japan. In that sense, Glissant very much expanded my perception of this kind of rhizomatic thinking.

When I came back to my country twenty-one years ago, it felt like I was rediscovering it as an outsider.

It was familiar yet new and quite different, and I had to develop my own narrative in that context, drawing from early Korean pioneers, such as Kim Swoo Geun and Kim Chung-up. I also got to discover my neighbours such as Southeast and South Asia through figures whom I didn't know much about, including William Lim, Geoffrey Bawa, Vann Molyvann, Leandro Locsin, Wang Da Hong, to name a few. Again, thanks to you, discovering Glissant felt like finding the philosopher/poet counterpart for these architects.

In the centre of your Pavilion is a void evoking the *madang*, a versatile courtyard space often present in traditional Korean houses. Can you tell me more about that?

Traditional Korean *madang*. Jeong Si-yeong's House, Hwaseong, Korea. Courtesy of the Korean Heritage Service

Many cultures and eras have the residential typology with courtyards, but Korean *madangs* are probably the most profoundly empty. This quality likely stems from a Zen tradition and the advent of Buddhism, where an empty podium, without Buddha, was celebrated. However, it's also a very environmental and pragmatic idea. It's almost forbidden by custom to plant anything in the *madang*. Instead, it is left with the brightest dirt to reflect sunlight back into the surrounding interior spaces. This also creates a microclimate for ventilation and humidity control. This nothingness without a prescribed programme allows everyday, individual household activities to take place as well as large collective gatherings like wedding ceremonies. I also refer to this void in our pavilion as an anticlimax. Often in Western architecture, such as the Palladian rotunda, the climax is at the centre. In contrast, the edges of the central *madang* features the lowest overhang of the timber roof, creating the most intimate space with the sky above, instead of having a constructed sky or heaven at the centre.

Our Pavilion's *madang* is not a very controlled space but one that forces you to constantly walk around and

Program scenario diagrams, Serpentine Pavilion 2024 *Archipelagic Void*. Image courtesy of Mass Studies

where things happen. What we've created is a place with very diverse qualities through five 'islands' hosting different programmes. Furthermore, these five spaces created five in-between open spaces, all around a central void. In the end there are eleven boundless spaces with distinctive characters that invite people to walk around and explore.

This *madang* frames the surrounding landscape without trying to control too much, leaving it undefined. At the opening reception of the Pavilion, I observed how most people gravitated towards the centre of the void, while very few were standing at the back. Taking inspiration from Frederick Law Olmsted's vision of achieving a 'commonplace civilisation' in designing the Central Park in New York, our interest lies in creating inclusive spaces for an 'organised gregariousness', also

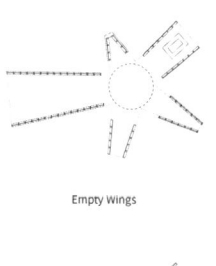

Empty wings

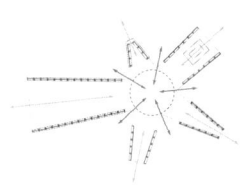

View through each wings & in-between spaces

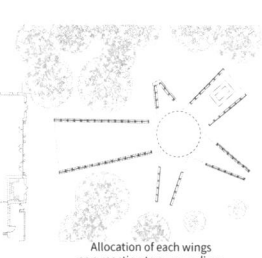

Allocation of each wings as a reaction to surroundings

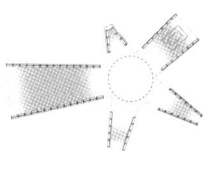

Each wing provides spaces that are more enclosed and quieter

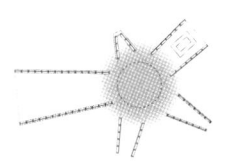

The cantilevered structure allows for open views through amongst the wings.

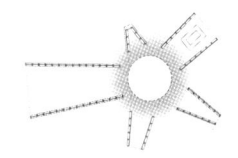

Flexible space contained within the defined structure

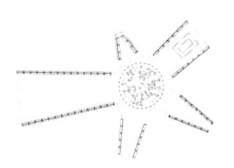

88 people standing / 44 people sitting

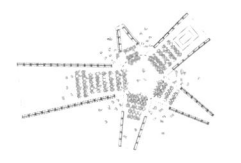

618 people standing / 309 people sitting
In nice weather, there is opportunity to occupy the spaces in-between the wings.

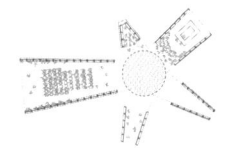

164 people standing / 82 people sitting

a term he coined. At Mass Studies, we refer to this concept as 'collective intimacy'. This pursuit is particularly crucial in a world where diversity is highly valued yet compartmentalised, with increasing seductions to remain mere spectators rather than actively engaging in voluntary participation.

I'm very interested in this aspect of your Pavilion, the idea of togetherness and having places where we can gather without being forced to consume — an architecture for everyone. In an increasingly polarised world, where social media is creating isolation instead of togetherness, that's one of the important things architecture and art can do. Your pavilion is inspired by traditional Korean ways of living, where we have a more tactile relationship with architecture. Tell me about the connection to Korean tradition and the sensitivity to materials you chose to create this multi-sensory experience.

I think architecture is the only non-downloadable thing that we still have. Our Pavilion is trying to embody that by creating a tactile experience through *The Library of Unread Books* by Heman Chong and Renée Staal. Additionally it engages the other senses such as taste and smell in the *Tea House*, and of course, hearing through Jang Young-Gyu's soundscape in the *Gallery*, as well as the larger events held in the *Auditorium*. The *Play Tower* brings a full bodily experience.

    The overall design and construction is, on one hand, inspired by traditional Korean architecture. However, like Gottfried Semper's four elements of architecture,[1] exemplified by his analysis of the primitive hut, I believe it possesses qualities that people from various cultures can easily engage with and make associations in their own meaningful way. Koreans probably have the most tactile relationship with architecture. We remove our shoes when we go inside and often sleep while hugging

[1]. In his book *The Four Elements of Architecture*, Gottfried Semper identified the four distinct elements as the hearth, the roof, the enclosure and the mound.

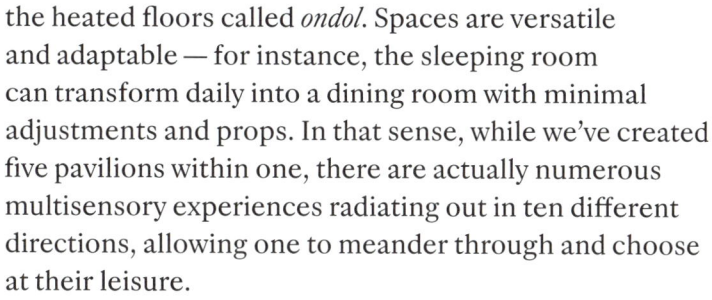

the heated floors called *ondol*. Spaces are versatile and adaptable — for instance, the sleeping room can transform daily into a dining room with minimal adjustments and props. In that sense, while we've created five pavilions within one, there are actually numerous multisensory experiences radiating out in ten different directions, allowing one to meander through and choose at their leisure.

We chose natural Douglas fir timber as the main material, a quite basic material that Koreans have used in the past and also in any location. Here, it comes from Surrey, only thirty kilometres away. However, the way we organised and assembled it is quite sophisticated and intricate, involving digital fabrication. The parametric timber work involves 350 uniquely designed steel joints for the *Auditorium* alone, because of how the structure flares outwards. As mentioned in Semper's primitive hut, the use of a wood structure on stone plinths is also well-rooted in Western architecture and British tradition, and can be seen in granary constructions, to keep dampness and insects out of the grain. It's also a method that's used beyond England. We've combined these traditional systems and materials with modern ones such as low-carbon concrete, recyclable polycarbonate and PVC membrane.

Can you expand further on the idea of the Pavilion being both site specific and site-less?

Site specific is about creating a dialogue and connecting with the surroundings on various scales. Urbanistically, our Pavilion works as a roundabout for pedestrian park activities connecting with surrounding passages and roads. Architecturally, the five wings or 'islands' are carefully positioned between the trees in the Serpentine South lawn. Also the Pavilion interacts with the Serpentine South building in various ways experienced

Buseoksa Temple, 676 (reconstructed in 1376), in Yeongju, North Gyeongsang Province, Korea. Photo by Yong-Kwan Kim

The Red Devils gathered in front of Seoul City Hall and around the traffic roundabout during the 2002 FIFA World Cup (due to this public phenomena it has now been transformed into Seoul Plaza), in Seoul, South Korea

Site plan, Serpentine Pavilion 2024 *Archipelagic Void*. Image courtesy of Mass Studies

from various positions. It's quite a 'contextual pavilion', as some might find contradictory. On a smaller human body scale, we took advantage of the discovery that the Pavilion site is not a flat ground but a very gentle slope from west to east for water drain. We created a datum with lower beams to accommodate different body sizes, with benches in varying heights and counters for the *Library* and *Tea House*. Our Pavilion can be understood as ten walls with benches at varying heights, that are covered or uncovered, radiating in ten different directions.

From the outside, each 'island' has a very different character, from wide to narrow, low to tall, big to small, but from the central *madang*, they're all completed with exactly the same element, a floating arc built at the lowest legally possible height that makes up one fifth of the eight-metre-diameter circle. 'Site-lessness' comes out of this aspect. This allows the five 'islands' to be re-assembled in up to 120 different variations. We

120 plan variations, Serpentine Pavilion 2024 *Archipelagic Void*. Image courtesy of Mass Studies

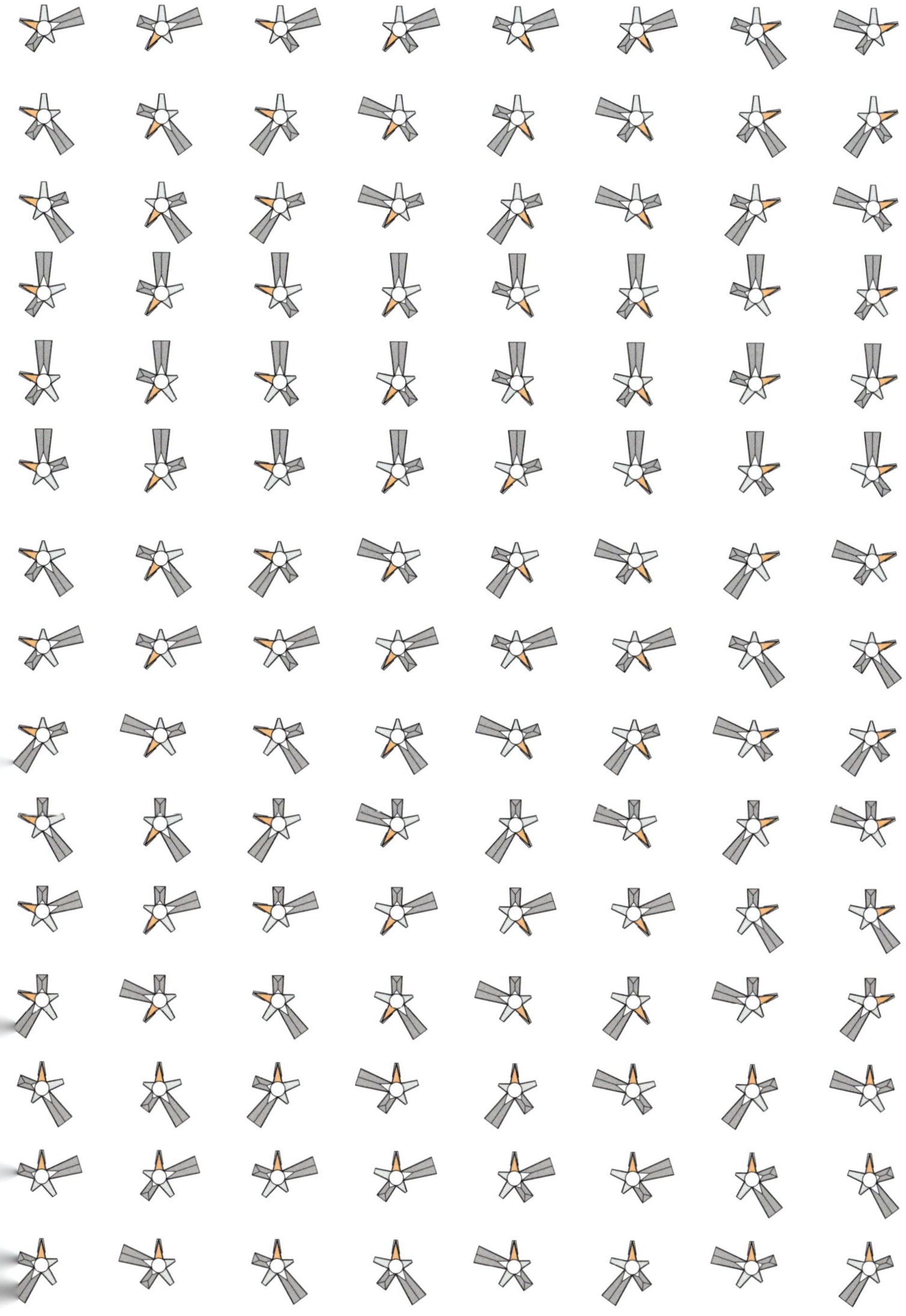

ISO view of the five 'islands' of the Pavilion at the center (top) and periphery (bottom). Image courtesy of Mass Studies

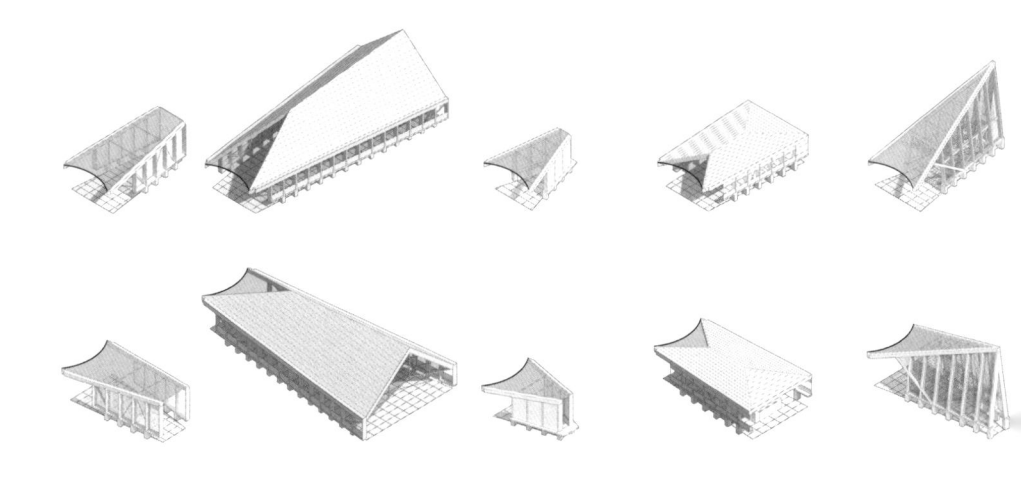

don't know where the Pavilion will go after its life on the Serpentine lawn, but it can be rearranged to respond to the unknown conditions of the future site. In the end, our Pavilion is an amalgamation of our discoveries and inventive processes, using simultaneous contextual and conceptual approaches that blend the traditional Korean pavilion with the Western folly to create the unexpected.

What else is happening in your office right now?

At the moment, I'm excited about three public projects. All of them are under construction. One of them is the Seoul Film Centre, previously known as the Seoul Cinematheque, located in Chungmu-ro. This building is situated in the heart of South Korea's domestic film industry and where the country's first cinema was established. In 2011, some of the most prominent figures in the Korean film industry such as film directors Park Chan-wook and Bong Joon-ho advocated for creating a publicly funded art-house cinema. The result is a forty-metre-tall building that extends twenty metres underground, vertically arranged with three cinemas, a library archive, an editing room, community spaces

Rendering of the Seoul Film Center (under construction, expected completion 2025), in Seoul, South Korea. Image courtesy of Mass Studies

Renderings of the Yeonhui Public Housing (under construction), in Seoul, South Korea. Image courtesy of Mass Studies

Model of the Danginri Cultural Power Plant (under construction), in Seoul, South Korea. Photo by Yousub Song

and much more. The second is a unique public-housing project. Located near universities, this residential building consists of 100 apartments designed as an incubator for young adults. It includes shared workspaces and a gym open to the community, all built on top of public infrastructure for flood prevention known as a water pump station. The third project is an appropriation of a former power plant, which includes our latest pavilion called the Hyper Pavilion. Construction began a few months ago. This will be another cultural project with a small budget, yet the purpose and potential are very significant.

Can you describe the Hyper Pavilion in more detail?

The Seoul Power Station, Korea's first-ever thermoelectric power plant, was built in 1930 by the Han River. Two of the units built in the 1970s were shut down as power generation moved underground, beneath the adjacent park, leaving them vacant. One of these units will be preserved as an industrial historic relic, with all the boilers and turbine machines intact for people to learn about its history. The 'organs' of the other unit are being completely gutted out to transform it into a new public space, and together form the new Danginri Cultural Power Plant. This space utilises almost 90% of the existing structures, creating the best viewing spot for the river and an events space on what we call the 'podium'— a new public space located eighteen metres above the ground created by combining the two rooftops together. The Hyper Pavilion sits on top of the podium, utilises structures and catwalks left after gutting one of the boilers. We've just added a lightweight roof on top of it. It can be understood as a 'found fun palace', referencing Cedric Price.

What's your advice to a young architect in 2024?

I've been asked this before, and what I said then was, 'Don't listen to an old guy like me.' I'd also add, 'Do your own thing and be kind to others.' But now I'll say this: focus on doing two seemingly opposite things well. First, you have to remember that you're a special person and that special thing you have is needed in this world — you have to hold onto it forever. Second, keep in mind that, at the same time, you're not *that* special. That way you won't be an isolated island but will connect with others to create an archipelago of ideas that will expand you.

This catalogue is published
to accompany the
Serpentine Pavilion 2024
Archipelagic Void designed by
Minsuk Cho, Mass Studies,
7 June–27 October 2024

Serpentine Pavilion 2024
© Minsuk Cho, Mass Studies

Edited by Alexa Chow,
Gonzalo Herrero Delicado
and Yesomi Umolu
Copyedited by Melissa Larner
Translation from Korean by
Emily Jungmin Yoon
Designed by Sulki & Min
Printed by Gomer Press in
Wales, UK

First published in 2024 by
Serpentine and Verlag der
Buchhandlung Walther und
Franz König, Köln

© 2024 Minsuk Cho,
Mass Studies; Serpentine,
London; the authors;
and Verlag der Buchhandlung
Walther und Franz König, Köln

All rights reserved. No part
of this publication may
be reproduced, stored
in a retrieval system or
transmitted in any form or
by any means, electronic,
mechanical, photocopying,
recording or otherwise
without prior permission of
the publishers. The publishers
of this book are committed
to respecting the intellectual
property rights of others.
Every effort has been made
to trace copyright holders and
to obtain their permission for
the use of copyright material.
The publishers apologise
for any errors or omissions
in the above list and would
be grateful if notified of any
corrections that should be
incorporated in future reprints
or editions of this book.

Published by

SERPENTINE

Serpentine
Kensington Gardens
London W2 3XA
Telephone +44 (0) 207 402 6075
Fax +44 (0) 207 402 4103
www.serpentinegalleries.org

Verlag der Buchhandlung
Walther und Franz Konig
Ehrenstr. 4
D-50672 Köln

Bibliographic information
published by the Deutsche
Nationalbibliothek. The
Deutsche National-bibliothek
lists this publication in the
Deutsche Nationalbibliografie;
detailed bibliographic data are
available on the Internet at
http://dnb.d-nb.de.

Distribution

Europe
Buchhandlung Walther König
Ehrenstr. 4
D-50672 Köln
Telephone +49 (0) 221 / 20 59 6 53
verlag@buchhandlung-walther-koenig.de

UK & Ireland
ART DATA
12 Bell Industrial Estate
50 Cunnington Street
London W4 5HB
United Kingdom
Telephone +44 (0)208 747 10 61
Fax +44 (0)208 742 23 19
orders@artdata.co.uk

Outside Europe
D.A.P. / Distributed Art Publishers, Inc.
75 Broad Street, Suite 630
USA – New York, NY 10004
Telephone +1 (0) 212 627 1999
orders@dapinc.com

ISBN 978-1-908617-86-6
Serpentine, London

ISBN 978-3-7533-0688-9
Verlag der Buchhandlung
Walther und Franz König, Köln

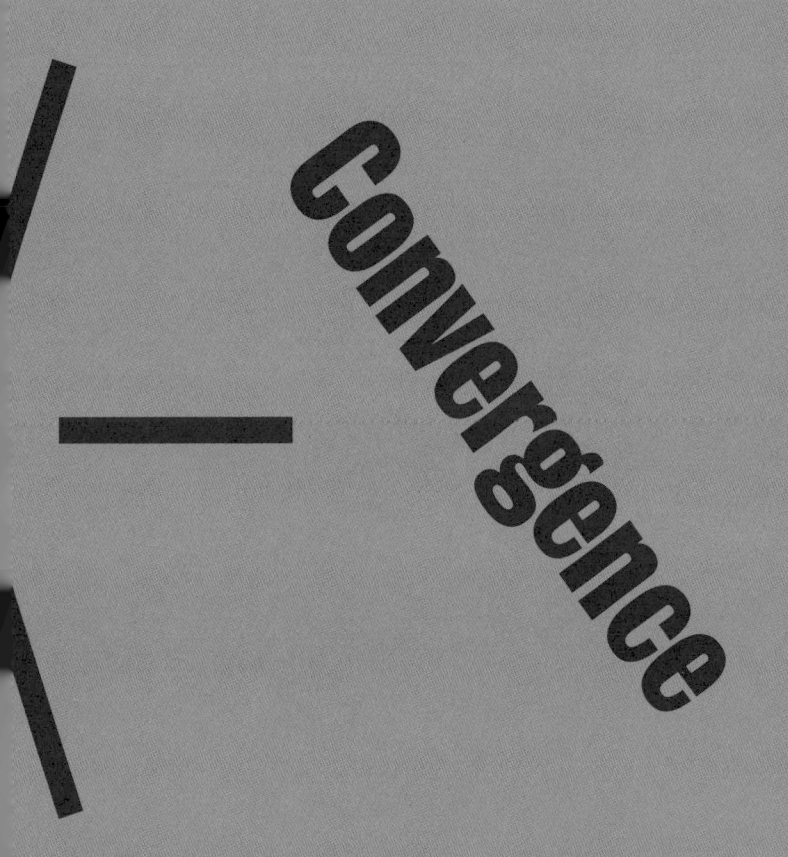

Serpentine Pavilion 2024
Archipelagic Void
Mass Studies

Convergence

Serpentine Pavilion 2024 Archipelagic Void   Mass Studies

Edited by
Alexa Chow, Gonzalo Herrero Delicado
and Yesomi Umolu

Convergence

Alex Taek-Gwang Lee	The Void of Archipelagic Planetarity	2
Renée Green	Seeing and Hearing Works Together in Space	12
Beatrice Galilee	Pavilion Is Pavilion Is Not Pavilion	20
Eun-Me Ahn	Mincho FiveStar Dance in the Chomin Suksuk Night, Groove and NoFluke Beats, Rising Rhythms of Unexpected Skies, Mincho Mix and Star Dance Disguise, Feel the Transforming Vibe of Suksuk Chomin, Twirl in the Night, Reach for the Rhythms, Starry Skies and Dance Shifts	26
Jang Young-Gyu	*The Willow Is* 〈버들은〉 and *Moonlight* 〈월정명〉	30

Alex Taek-Gwang Lee
The Void of Archipelagic Planetarity

While Korea is geographically situated on a peninsula, its ideological stance has often isolated it from mainstream global perspectives, akin to an island detached from the mainland. This divergence manifested starkly after the nation's division, as North and South Korea embarked on distinct modernisation paths, guided by contrasting ideological doctrines of socialism and capitalism respectively. In this way, no matter which Korea they are born in, Koreans must choose from one set of values or the other. The more the reality of division is reinforced, the more the possibility of other choices disappears.

    Minsuk Cho's return to this impasse in 2001 can be seen as a pivotal moment, when he reemerges from the confines of the grand narrative of the 'refugee'. According to his testimony, this decision was not arbitrary; rather, it was a compelling necessity driven by circumstances that had already set the stage for a profound transformation at the dawn of the twenty-first century.[1] He considered his homeland as a desert island where he could rejuvenate his vision. This vague belief proved to be naïve: the imagined shelter turned out to be a resting ground for shipwrecks, perpetually delivered by the relentless ebb and flow of the tide.

1. Minsuk Cho, 'The Heterogeneity and Commonality of Won Buddhism Wonnam Temple', *Winner of the 5th KAAH Design Award* (Seoul: Gedaerolab, 2023), p. 57.

This observation ultimately led Cho to reflect on the place to which he had returned. His profound experience served as the catalyst behind the inception of his exhibition at the 14th International Architecture Exhibition — la Biennale di Venezia, 2014, where he represented South Korea and received the prestigious Golden Lion Award.

Cho took the exhibition title *Crow's Eye View* from a line by Korean poet, Yi Sang (1910–1937), who had a background in architecture. At first glance, it might seem as if Cho was trying to attain a bird's-eye perspective on the realities unfolding on the Korean Peninsula. However, such an assumption would be a mistake as a 'crow's eye view' is not the same as a 'bird's-eye view'. Cho goes deeper into Yi Sang's poetic torsion on this matter. What exactly is a 'crow's eye view'? It is not merely a top-down contemplation of metaphysical concepts: it grants us insight from the opposite angle. Cho's perspective strives to reveal the reverse side of his country from beneath. In this sense, Cho's architecture seeks to crack open the self-containment of Korean modernity. Since the 1960s, Korea has been dominated by the logic of compressed modernisation, which has manifested in both North and South in an extreme form of European modernist aesthetic. This approach internalises natural spaces by fragmenting and isolating them. Korea's modernisation process has produced, for example, apartments that look as if they have been manufactured in a factory.

In order to vividly demonstrate this intensive

modernisation, Cho introduces the concept of cartography as a method to see the world in a more holistic way. However, this notion of cartography differs from the two-dimensional flat representations we commonly encounter in aerial photography and satellite imagery today. Instead, his intricate art of mapping is a performative map of the senses, reminiscent of explorers traversing a terrain on foot. This synthesis of the senses deconstructs the geometry of surveillance. The underlying principle here overcomes the traditional dichotomy between culture and nature to embrace our inherent interconnectedness with the natural world. This concept forms the bedrock of Cho's work. Seamlessly blending nature and the built environment, his unique cartographic approach also finds expression in structures like the 2010 Shanghai Expo Korean Pavilion and Daum Space 1. Rather than imposing dominating forms that overpower their surroundings, these buildings integrate harmoniously with the landscape, becoming an extension of their setting instead of asserting an overpowering architectural identity.

His approach to cartography can be likened to archaeology. In his retrospective analysis of the design process for the Won Buddhism Wonnam Temple, he uncovers a forgotten circular topography obscured by urban development and situates the architecture within that curvature. This cartographic method resembles an archaeological dig, revealing layers of history and meaning embedded in the

Daum Space.1, 2011, in Jeju
Province, South Korea.
Photo by Yong-Kwan Kim

Won Buddhism Wonnam
Temple, 2022, in
Seoul, South Korea.
Photo by Mass Studies

Unidenfied artist,
Banquet Celebrating the 6oth Wedding Anniversary,
18th century. Ink and color on silk, 33.5 × 45.5 cm.
© National Museum of Korea

landscape. By reframing the temple not as an isolated entity but as a space interconnected with its surroundings, he aims to transcend the conventional notion of sacredness confined within its enclosed walls. He seeks to integrate and elevate the diverse heterogeneity of the external world, where secular elements converge, offering a broader perspective on spirituality and human existence. To achieve this, the nomadic architect uncovers the essence of Korean spatiality known as *madang* (마당). This concept, which defies easy translation into English as simply a yard or garden, encapsulates a unique form with a distinctive usage. Unlike conventional spaces, *madang* is not predefined on blueprints; instead, it materialises within the interstitial spaces between buildings only when the initial plan has been completed. This substantial space functions as a connecting thread between buildings, akin to a group of islands in the Mediterranean Sea, each with its distinct purpose and yet unified by the surrounding expanse.

    The design of Cho's Serpentine Pavilion, aptly titled *Archipelagic Void*, embodies this architectural philosophy. The open *madang* at its core prevents the spaces that extend in various directions from feeling isolated. Much like the ocean that unites islands, this space brims with potential and connectivity, offering endless possibilities. As Édouard Glissant writes, 'it is a sea of fundamental chasm, of an internal abyss that determines all philosophies of the One'.[2]

    Cho's Pavilion challenges the notion of a monolithic, continent-centred modernity by

2. Édouard Glissant, *The Baton Rouge Interviews*, trans. Kate M. Cooper (Liverpool: Liverpool University Press, 2020), p. 57.

Seyeonjeong Pavilion,
c. 1637, Bogildo Island,
Wando County, South Jeolla
Province, South Korea.
Photo by Bumhyun Chun

embodying the essence of the archipelago. This defiance introduces the principle of 'seascape' as an alternative to the geometric landscape inherent in highly modern architecture. His expression goes beyond the narrow sense of reason grounded in mathematical calculations, instead embracing a broader rationality: the realisation of relational poetics.

The Serpentine Pavilion 2024 stands as the culmination of myriad experiences garnered since Cho's return to the homeland, when his approach to Korean aesthetics coalesced into a vivid imagination shaped by his deep-rooted understanding of his country. Here, the fusion of traditional Korean architecture with an international grammar unfolds, ushering in new aesthetic realms. The Pavilion's design, particularly its roof and asymmetrical structure, pays homage to the rich tapestry of traditional Korean architecture. An integral facet of this tradition lies in the distinctive construction of windows and doors, where the natural elements outside seamlessly meld with the exterior walls. Rather than imposing structures that separate internal space from the external environment, these architectural features engender an ambivalent spatiality, where the outside environment harmoniously intertwines with the inside. However, Cho's aspirations extend beyond the mere modernisation of traditional forms; he infuses them with a transformative conceptual essence, eliciting a poetic imagination and inviting participatory engagement. Consequently, his architecture serves as a conduit for exploring and expressing the depths of poetic performance.

Cho's idea of architecture entails integrating nature into culture rather than constructing cultural edifices from natural elements. For him, architecture is not about the structuring of technical objects but about leaving the void, the points of boundaries that cannot converge into one. This void is empty, devoid of structure, yet full, since it encompasses all possibilities. The asymmetrical relations of the structure and their inherent variations facilitate the creation of this void. This exemplifies the archipelagic ontology embodied in Cho's Serpentine Pavilion, an ontology that fosters subjectivities that re-imagine the planet beyond the total computation that operates on a global scale.

As Gayatri Chakravorty Spivak says, 'we cannot turn planetarity into the production of an adjective for ourselves'.[3] The imperative of our planet demands that we rethink its essence. Cho's work offers an architectural response to the question: how can we envision the planet anew? He aims to forge a space capable of organising fragmented individuals into a collective subjectivity devoid of a singular centre. There is an ever-present risk that a global, all-encompassing representation or worldview might create a distorted reality detached from the physical world. In constructing such overarching narratives, we may overlook the Earth itself, echoing the concerns and anxieties expressed by modernist thinkers.

3. Gayatri Chakravorty Spivak and Susanne M. Winterling, 'The imperative to make the imagination flexible', *Planetary Sensing*, https://planetarysensing.com/the-imperative-to-make-the-imagination-flexible/.

Embracing the concept and practice of planetary imagination becomes crucial in navigating our relationship with the planet itself. This approach acknowledges the Earth's uniqueness while guarding against the persistent and misleading temptation of scientific overreach, wherein our models and theories might make unfounded claims to fully capture the complexity of our world. Cho opts to relinquish control over the architectural space, embracing its inherent complexity not through overcrowding but by stripping it to reveal its openness.

A diagrammatic shape like a pavilion seamlessly aligns with Cho's architectural ethos, showcasing how the juxtaposition of 'planetarity-archipelago' against the backdrop of 'globality-continent' can offer alternative spatial paradigms. This approach fosters a fresh perspective on the interpretation of space, diverging from the homogenising forces of globalisation and comprising the singularity and fragmentation inherent in our planetary reality. Through this emptying of the space, Cho invites us to contemplate the Earth's intricate multiplicities, prompting us to rethink our connection with the planet beyond oversimplified, all-encompassing narratives.

Alex Taek-Gwang Lee is a professor of cultural studies and a founding director of the Centre for Technology in Humanities at Kyung Hee University, Korea. He is also a visiting professor at the Centre for Applied Philosophy, Politics and Ethics at the University of Brighton (UK) and Graduate School at The University of Santo Tomas (The Philippines). He served as an academic advisor for Gwangju Biennale in 2017 and as a program manager for the Venice Biennale of Architecture in 2021. He is currently a board member of The International Consortium of Critical Theory Programs (ICCTP) and Asia Theories Network (ATN). He edited the third volume of *The Idea of Communism* (2016) and *Deleuze, Guattari and the Schizoanalysis of Postmedia* (2023).

Renée Green
Seeing and Hearing Works Together in Space

Renée Green is an artist, writer and filmmaker. Her exhibitions, videos and films have been seen throughout the world in art museums and institutions, biennales and film festivals. A selection of her books includes *Inevitable Distances* (2022), Pacing (2020) and *Other Planes of There: Selected Writings* (2014). She is the editor of *Negotiations in the Contact Zone* (2003) and a Professor on the Art, Culture and Technology programme at MIT, School of Architecture & Planning.

| There Is No Land Yet | 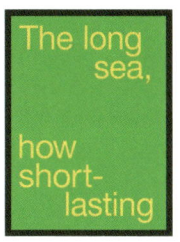 The long sea, how short-lasting |  From water-thought to water-thought |  So quick to feel surprise and shame |  Where moments are not time |

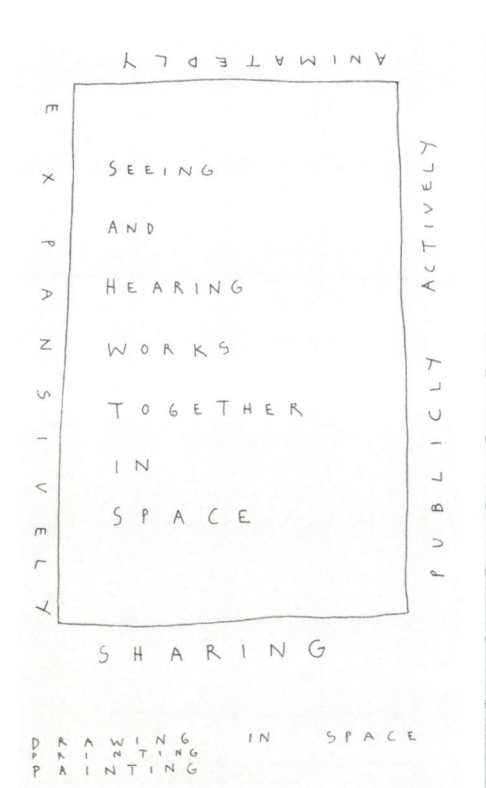

ANIMATEDLY

EXPANSIVELY

SEEING
AND
HEARING
WORKS
TOGETHER
IN
SPACE

PUBLICLY ACTIVELY

SHARING

DRAWING IN SPACE
PAINTING
PAINTING

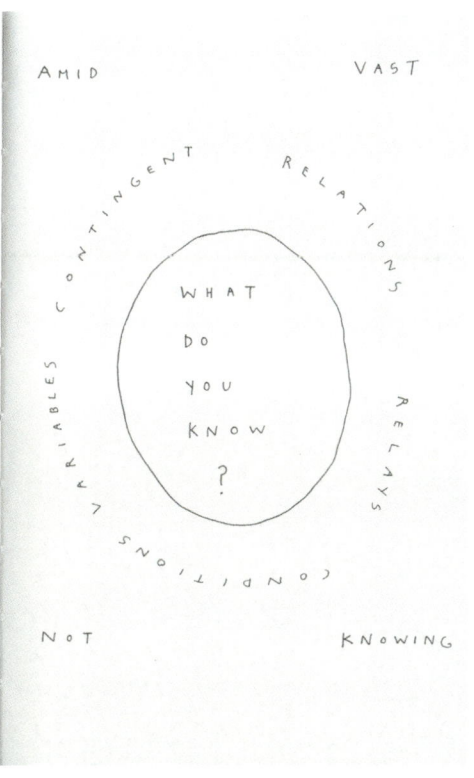

AMID   VAST

CONTINGENT RELATIONS

VARIABLES

WHAT
DO
YOU
KNOW
?

CONDITIONS RELAYS

NOT   KNOWING

| But time is moments |  Such neither yes nor no | 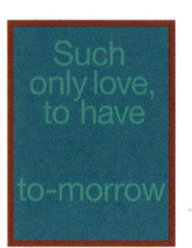 Such only love, to have to-morrow |  By certain failure of now and now. |  On water lying strong ships and men |

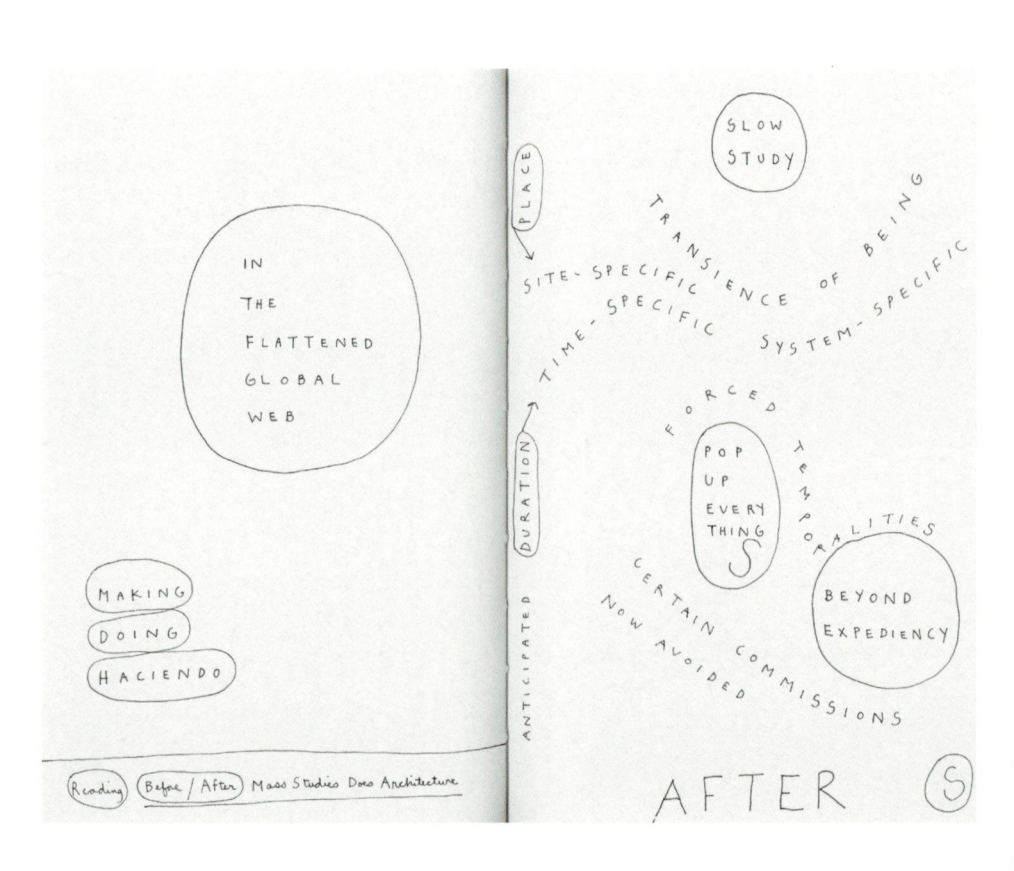

IN THE FLATTENED GLOBAL WEB

MAKING
DOING
HACIENDO

Reading (Before/After) Mass Studies Does Architecture

PLACE

DURATION

ANTICIPATED

SLOW STUDY

TRANSIENCE OF BEING
SITE-SPECIFIC   SYSTEM-SPECIFIC
TIME-SPECIFIC

FORCED TEMPORALITIES

POP UP EVERY THING

CERTAIN COMMISSIONS
NOW AVOIDED

BEYOND EXPEDIENCY

AFTER (S)

| In weakness skilled reach elsewhere: | 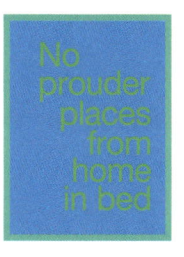 No prouder places from home in bed |  The mightiest sleeper can know. | 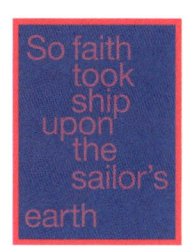 So faith took ship upon the sailor's earth |  To seek absurdities in heaven's name— |

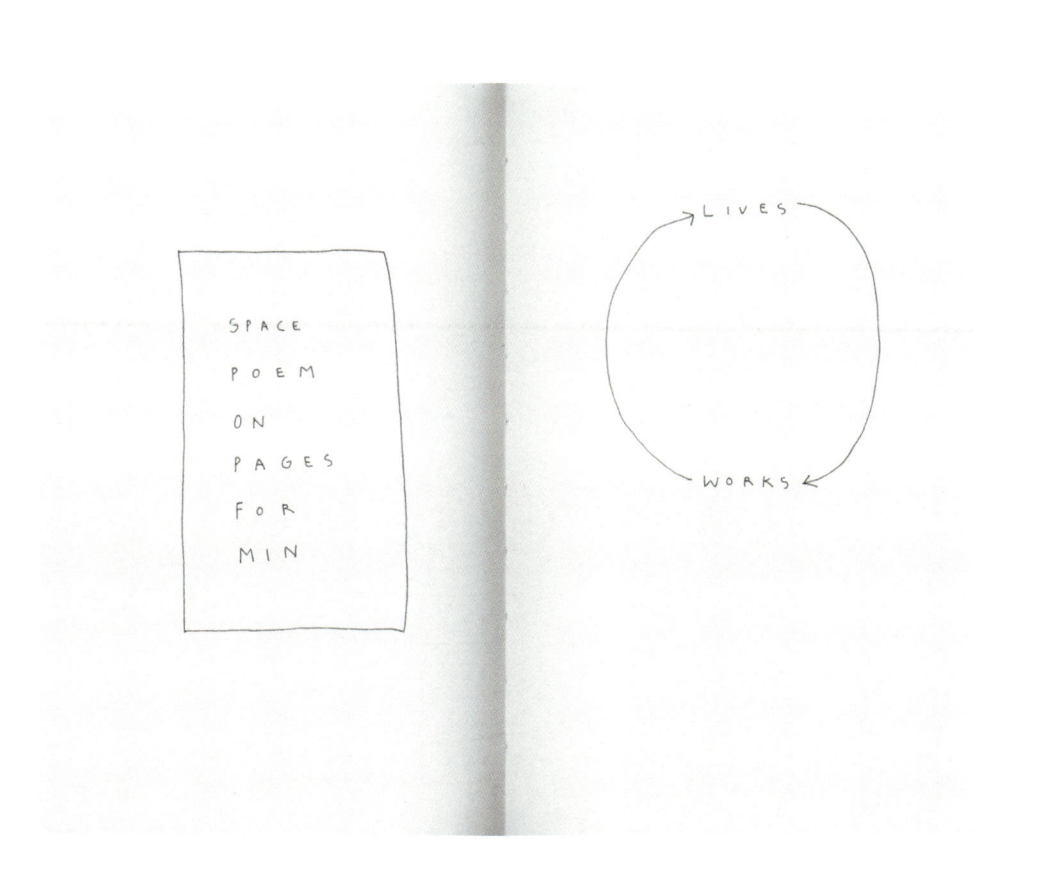

SPACE
POEM
ON
PAGES
FOR
MIN

→ LIVES
↑   ↓
← WORKS

Discovery but a fountain without source	Legend of mist and lost patience	The body swimming in itself	Is darling dissolution's	With dripping mouth it speaks a truth

PAGE　　　　　　　　SPACE

(PLACING)

　　　　SPACE　POEM　FOR　MIN

PLACE　　　　　　　PRESENCE

16

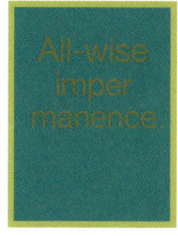

| That cannot lie, in words not born yet | Out of first immortality, | All-wise impermanence, | And the dusty eye whose accuracies | Turn watery in the mind |

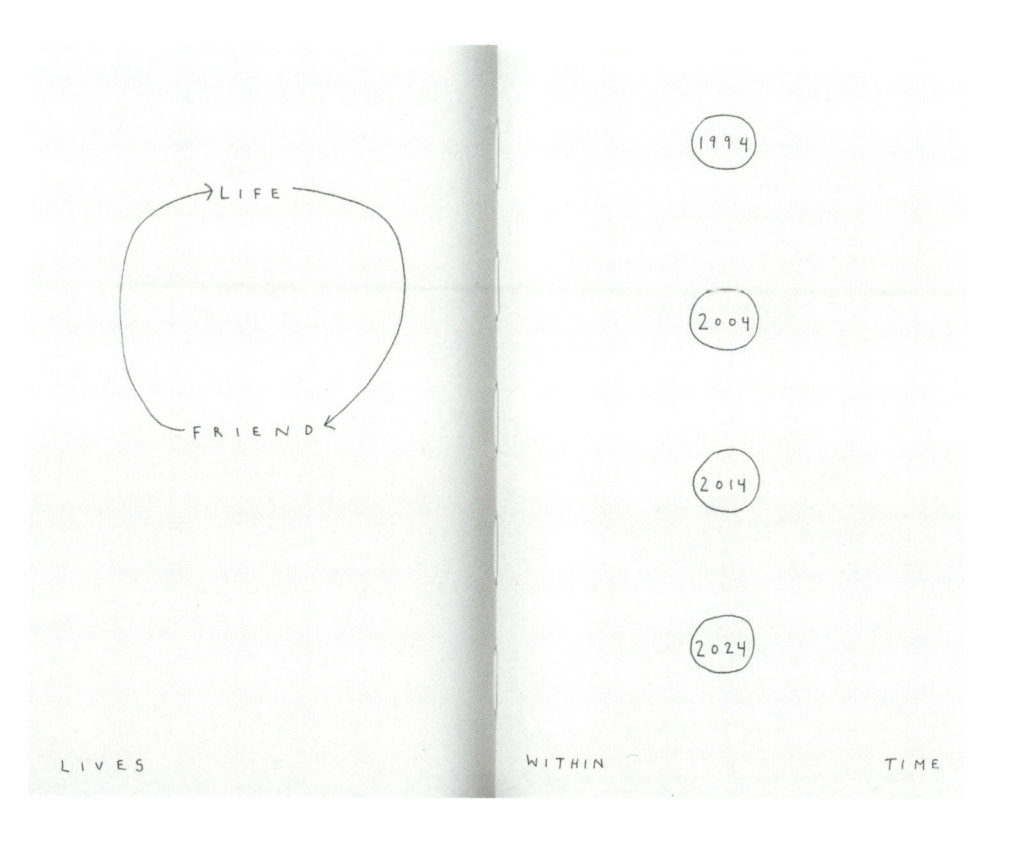

LIFE → FRIEND

1994

2004

2014

2024

LIVES　　　WITHIN　　　TIME

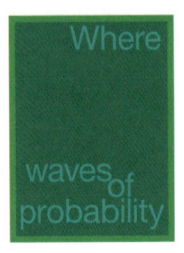

Where	Write	That	And	Lonely
waves of probability	vision in a tidal hand	time alone can read.	the dry land not yet,	and absolute salvation–

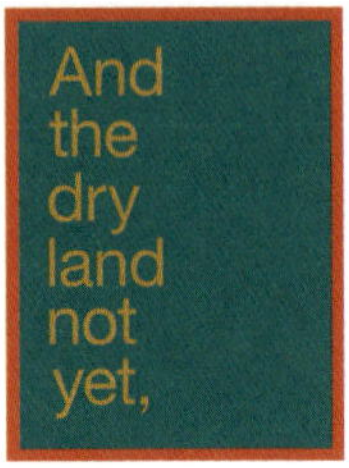

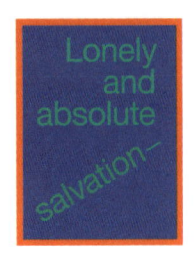

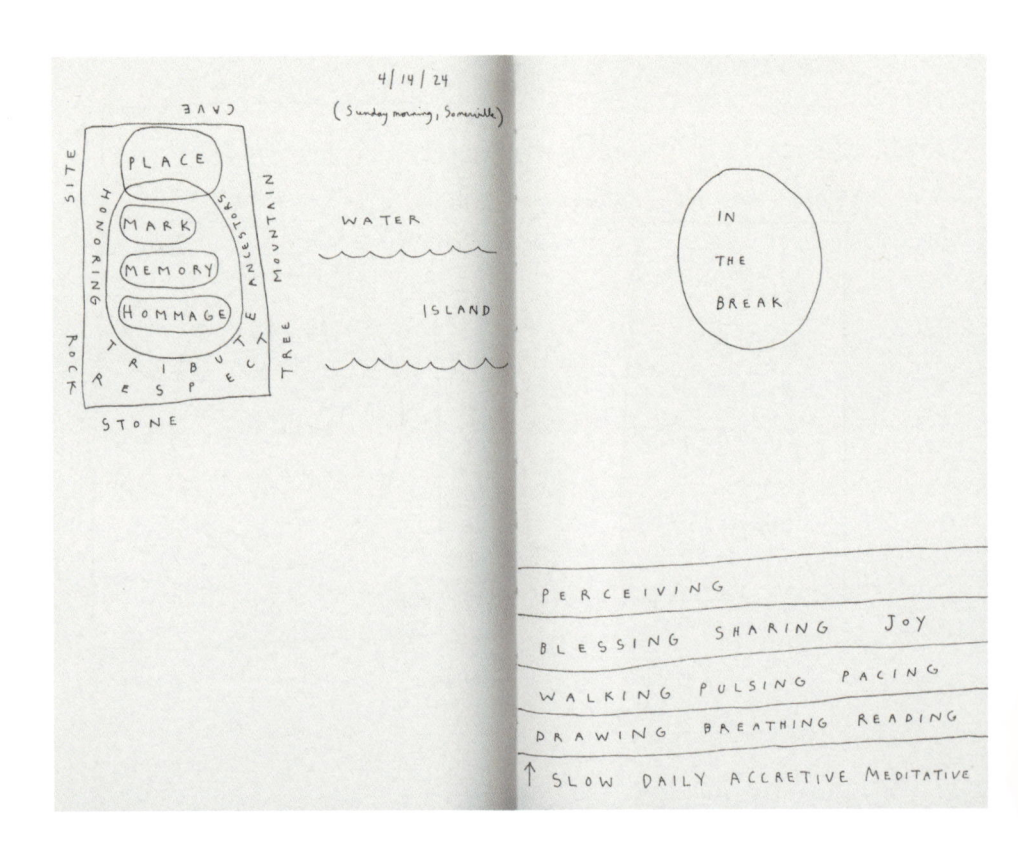

4/14/24
(Sunday morning, Somerville)

```
         CAVE
   ┌─────────────────┐
 S │  ╭─────╮      M │
 I │ H│PLACE│      O │
 T │ O╰─────╯ A    U │
 E │ N ╭────╮ N    N │ T
   │ O │MARK│ C    T │ R
 R │ R ╰────╯ E    A │ E
 O │ I╭──────╮S    I │ E
 C │ N│MEMORY│T    N │
 K │ G╰──────╯O      │
   │  ╭───────╮R     │
   │  │HOMMAGE│S     │
   │  ╰───────╯      │
   │    T R I B U T E│
   │   R E S P E C T │
   └─────────────────┘
       STONE
```

WATER
〜〜〜〜〜
ISLAND
〜〜〜〜〜

IN
THE
BREAK

PERCEIVING
BLESSING SHARING JOY
WALKING PULSING PACING
DRAWING BREATHING READING
↑ SLOW DAILY ACCRETIVE MEDITATIVE

Boasting of constancy

Like an island with no water round

In water where no land is.

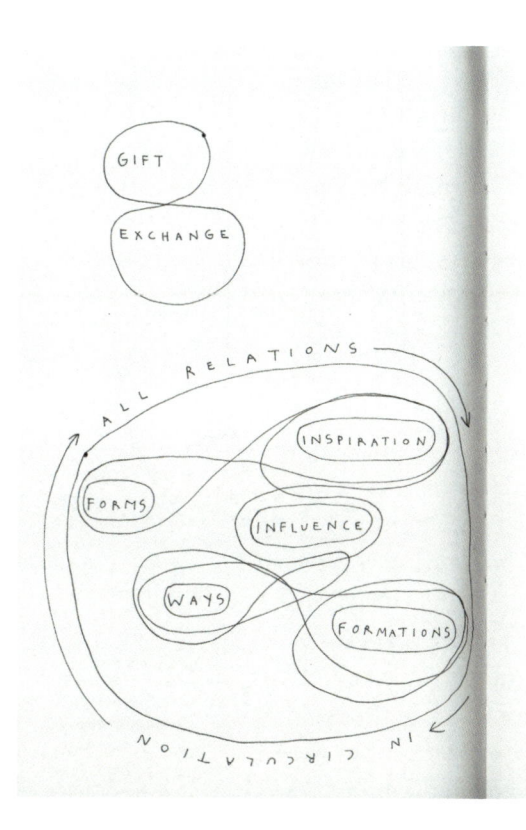

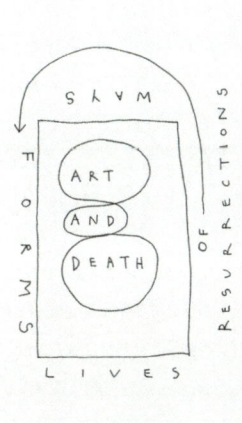

GIFT
EXCHANGE

ALL RELATIONS

INSPIRATION
FORMS
INFLUENCE
WAYS
FORMATIONS

IN CIRCULATION

FORMS
WAYS
ART AND DEATH
LIVES
RESURRECTIONS OF

Beatrice Galilee
Pavilion Is Pavilion Is Not Pavilion

For Minsuk Cho, the pavilion, a time-stamped and geo-located artefact of its time, is defined just as effectively by what it is not, as by what it is. In an expansive career that captivated the national and international community through museums, housing, infrastructure and more, it is Cho's ongoing commitment to interrogating and metabolising other forms of architectural culture from curatorial, artistic, performative and humane that differentiates him from most of the architects of his generation. *Archipelagic Void* perfectly responds to all of the best qualities of this multi-dimensional designer.

Cho's first role as a curator was working alongside artistic directors Ai WeiWei and Seung H-Sang for the 4th Gwangju Design Biennale in 2011. Inspired by the ancient Chinese philosophy of Lao-tzu's *Tao Te Ching*, 'The way (道) that is the way is not always the way', the artistic directors proposed a new variation — 'Design is Design is not Design' in English and *dogadobisangdo* (圖可圖非常圖, 도가도비상도) in Korean. Instead of showcasing hundreds of new design products, objects and design technologies for which Korea was becoming internationally renowned, the curators took the opportunity to entirely reevaluate the conventional understanding of the word 'design', presenting what it both is and is not, as a way of understanding the whole.

The two central curatorial sections were *Named*, led by Cho and Anthony Fontenot, and *Un-Named*, led by Brendan McGetrick. *Un-Named* focused on those areas of creativity and invention that are left out of the contemporary conversation on design, challenging the

Andrés Jaque / Office for Political Innovation, *Sweet Parliament Home*, presented at the 2011 Gwangju Design Biennale. Photo courtesy of the practice

Metahaven, *Transparent Camouflage — The Situation Is Catastrophic, But Not Serious (Slavoj Zizek)*, presented at the 2011 Gwangju Design Biennale. Photo by Kyungsub Shin

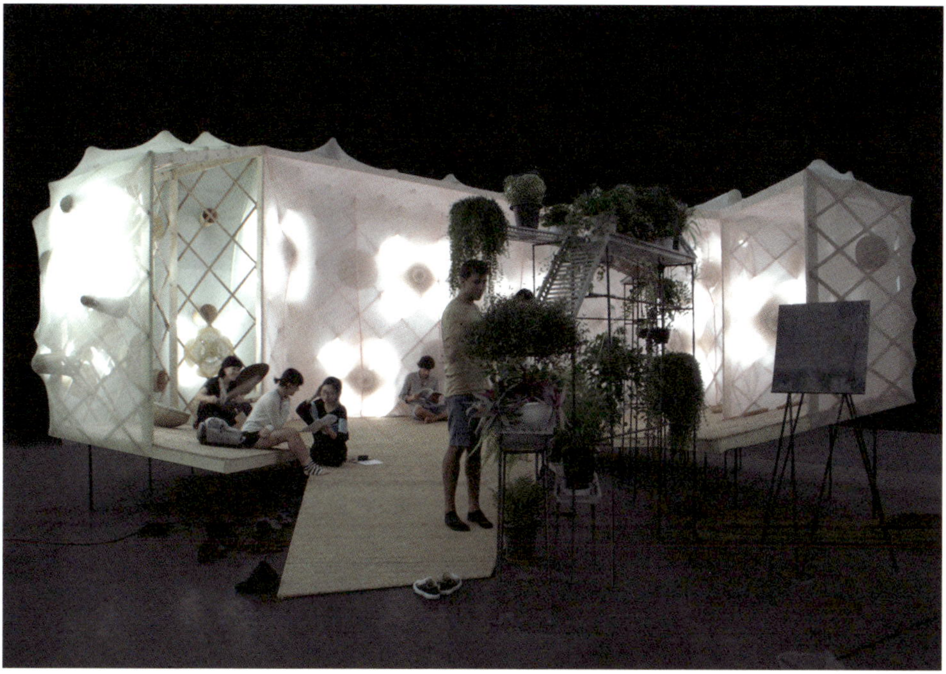

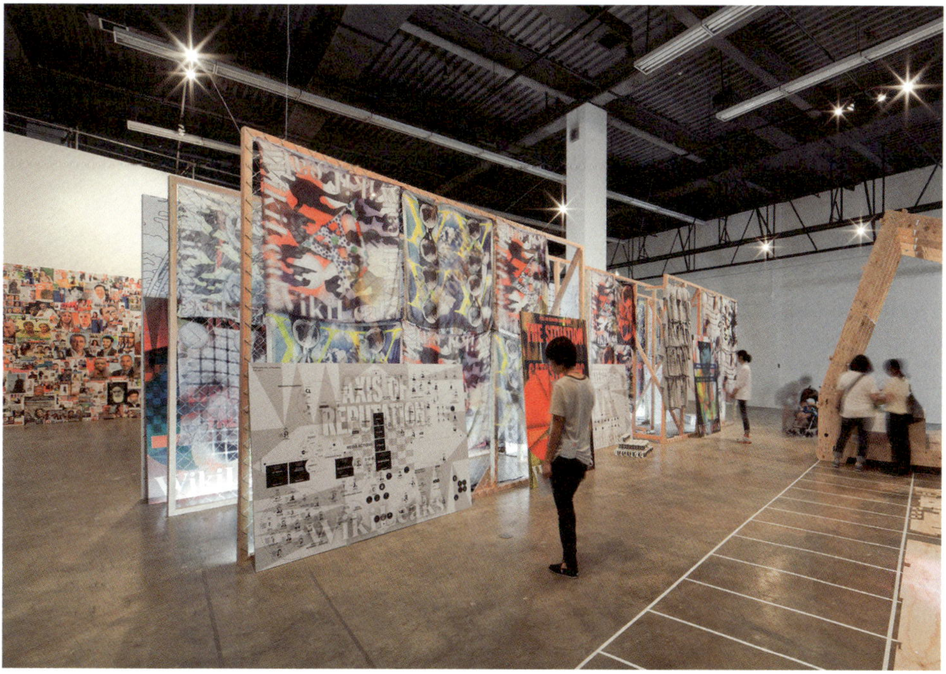

myth of the singular 'star designer' by including works that presented the design of athletes' bodies, genetic-modification techniques, low-cost healthcare, military technology and climate engineering to be examined and appreciated as contemporary design. On the other hand, Cho and Fontenot invited a thrilling spectrum of what constituted *Named* design at that time: commissioning Comme des Garçons's founder, Rei Kawakubo, to create a pavilion, and sharing new work by Joep van Lieshout, graphic designers Metahaven and Bruce Mau, fashion designers Henrik Vibskov and Andreas Emenius, iconic footwear company United Nude, an immersive installation with performance artist Eun-Me Ahn and another experimental pavilion by architect Andrés Jaque. There were also works by typographic designer Ahn Sang-soo, and parametric architect Michael Hansmeyer. The Biennale was reinforced by other curatorial projects, including a series of follies that were commissioned all over the Korean city of Gwangju. Despite its challenging content, the event was attended by over 700,000 people that year. As a curator, Cho brought complexity and creativity to the space, as well as a vision of the intellectual leadership role that Korea could play on the world stage of design.

    Before the 4th Gwangju Design Biennale in 2011, Cho focused both his major architectural accomplishments — including the Korea Pavilion at the Shanghai Expo 2010 — and his research interests, on the specificity of his country. As part of the curatorial team of the 2014 Korean Pavilion at the Venice Architecture Biennale, titled *Crow's Eye View: The Korean Peninsula*, Cho and his co-curators Hyungmin Pai and Changmo Ahn invited contributions from architects, artists, writers and filmmakers from North and South Korea that document the divergent post-war rebuilding of these neighbouring countries. The pavilion generated a kaleidoscopic narrative of these radically different reconstructions, in particular

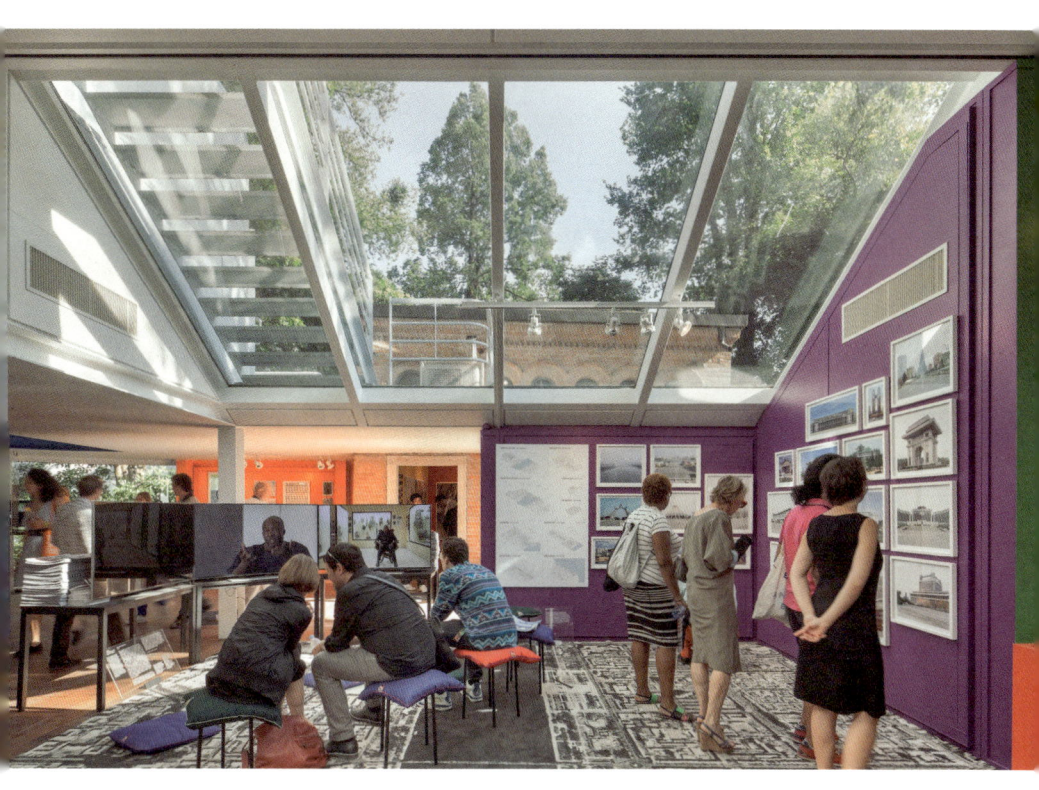

View of the exhibition
Crow's Eye View: The Korean Peninsula, 2014, at the Korean Pavilion in the 14th International Architecture Exhibition — la Biennale di Venezia in Venice, Italy. Photo by Kyungsub Shin

Yi Sang, *Crow's Eye View, Poem No. 4*, 1934. Typeset by Sulki & Min, 2014. Image by Sulki & Min

患者의容態에관한문제。

1234567890・
123456789・0
12345678・90
1234567・890
123456・7890
12345・67890
1234・567890
123・4567890
12・34567890
1・234567890
・1234567890

診斷 0・1
26・10・1931
以上 責任醫師 李箱

23

the illustrations, models, posters and photographs of a heavily militarised, monumental version of a North Korean utopia. Many of these images of the North were taken by internationals visiting the territory, not Korean nationals. The pavilion was awarded the prestigious Golden Lion for best national participation, the jury noting that the project was essentially a living, working document of a geopolitical reality in flux.

A prominent aspect of the exhibition in 2014 and in another solo work of Cho is a strip of land between North and South Korea, called the 'demilitarised zone' (DMZ). Completely abandoned since 1953, this no-man's land has long been the subject of cultural and political discourse. Over recent years, the possibility for a thawing of relations between north and south has seemed more attainable, and artists and architects have reimagined what the role of this land, untouched in nearly seventy years, could be.

Much of the fantasy around the DMZ is propelled by its extraordinary condition as an ecologically diverse environment, home to almost 2,000 different organisms, including nearly 100 endangered species. Cho's 2015 project *The DMZ Vault of Life and Knowledge* began as a contribution to the collective project *Dreaming of Earth ...* initiated in 2015 by artist Jae-Eun Choi in collaboration with architect Shigeru Ban. Jae-Eun Choi invited a group of artists, designers and architects, including Cho, to create a series of speculative projects that could envision a new life for the extraordinary landscape of the DMZ and as an essential starting point for the peaceful coexistence of the two Koreas. Cho's vision for a future seed bank and ecology library would enable both North and South Koreas to contribute to a shared purpose: to study, protect and nurture the ecology of the DMZ as a symbol of hope. Choi envisioned a seed bank at the northern entrance of the floating garden and an ecology library at the southern entrance. However, Cho proposed that these two symbiotic facilities could appropriate an existing tunnel of aggression that passes deep below the mountainous DMZ terrain. Like a kind of 'landscape acupuncture', it symbolises the relief of the divided land from decades of tension and allows for a flow of new energy.

Whether proposing a radical re-reading of the role of design, reconstructing communities in the aftermath of war or envisioning a sustainable future for the Korean Peninsula, Cho's work transcends the boundaries of traditional architecture, offering a compelling vision for the intersection of art, design and social change. These three projects would form the backbone of any international curator's career, yet for Cho, this work simply operates in perfect tandem, creating a kind of cultural armature within which he can operate a world-class architectural practice. In understanding Cho's approach to occupying the void that architecture creates, through exhibition-making, programming, art and life, we find not only the pavilion, but also what is not merely the pavilion, and a valuable contribution to a unique career and to architecture itself.

Beatrice Galilee is a curator, writer and design advisor based in New York. She is co-founder and chief curator of The World Around, an organisation dedicated to amplifying impactful and inspiring global architecture and design, and was the first curator of contemporary architecture and design at The Metropolitan Museum of Art. Her work includes serving as chief curator of the 2013 Lisbon Architecture Triennale, curator at the 2011 Gwangju Design Biennale, curator at the 2009 Shenzhen Hong Kong Biennale and co-founder and director of The Gopher Hole in London. She is a visiting professor at Pratt Institute and her writing has appeared in numerous publications. Galilee offers strategic advisory support to architects, designers and institutions, and is available for public speaking opportunities.

Eun-Me Ahn

Mincho FiveStar Dance in the Chomin Suksuk Night, Groove and NoFluke Beats, Rising Rhythms of Unexpected Skies, Mincho Mix and Star Dance Disguise, Feel the Transforming Vibe of Suksuk Chomin, Twirl in the Night, Reach for the Rhythms, Starry Skies and Dance Shifts

Eun-Me Ahn is a dancer born in Yeongju and raised in Seoul, South Korea, who became captivated by dance in her pre-school years. She began formal dance lessons in fifth grade and explored contemporary dance in middle school. In 1986, she debuted with *Siral*, followed by her first full-length production, *Paper Steps*, in 1988. Seeking greater challenges, she moved to New York, where she realised that the artistic potential she sought was already within her. Despite her exposure to contemporary dance, traditional Korean dance remained a core influence in her work.

Artistic Prompter: Eun-Me Ahn / Natural-Born AI: Kyungkyu Cho

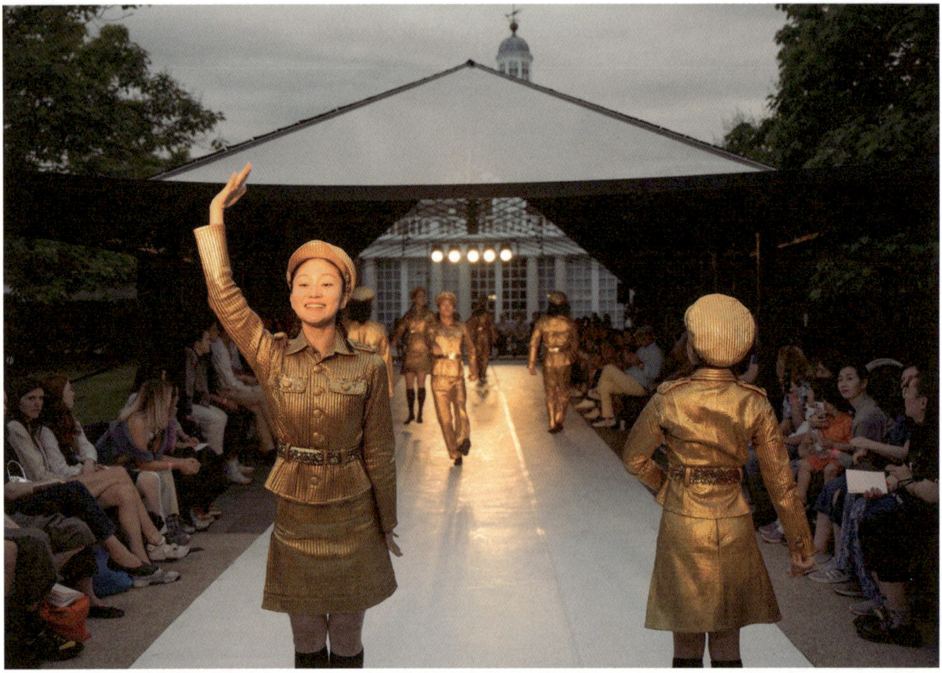

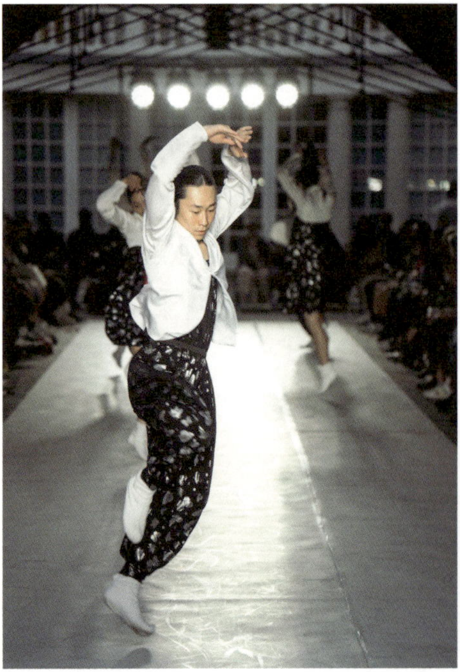

Park Nights is Serpentine's experimental, interdisciplinary live platform sited within the Pavilion. The 2024 *Park Nights* season kicked off with the UK premiere of *North Korea Dance* from renowned choreographer, Eun-Me Ahn and her dance company on Friday, 28 June and Saturday, 29 June. The piece explores the differences and similarities between North and South Korean dance and imagines a possible future beyond the border through shared movements. Bringing out the beauty in stark contrasts and celebrating the grotesque and the minimal, the subtle and the extreme, Eun-Me Ahn's compositions captivate audiences worldwide. For *Park Nights 2024*, Eun-Me invited audiences on an intimate journey to follow a dance between two divided nations.

Eun-Me Ahn, *North Korea Dance*,
part of Serpentine's *Park Nights 2024*.
Photo by Talie Rose Eigeland

Jang Young-Gyu

The Willow Is 〈버들은〉 and *Moonlight* 〈월정명〉

Jang Young-Gyu is a musician and composer who has worked with musical groups such as Uhuhboo Project, Be-Being and SsingSsing. He is currently a member of the band Leenalchi. Based in South Korea, his work seeks to create unconventional forms and techniques through exploring Korea's musical heritage in contemporary music. Jang also composes music for visual narratives and has provided scores for various South Korean blockbuster films and drama series such as *The Foul King* (2000), *Sympathy for Mr. Vengeance* (2002), *The Coast Guard* (2002), *Tazza: The High Rollers* (2006), *Train to Busan* (2016), *The Wailing* (2016) and *Alienoid* (2022).

As the main entry to the Serpentine Pavilion, the *Gallery* plays host to a six-channel sound installation created by South Korean musician and composer Jang Young-Gyu.

Taking inspiration from its surrounding environment, this new commission traces the changing of seasons and responds to the constantly transforming landscape and ecology of the park. *The Willow Is* 〈버들은〉 and *Moonlight* 〈월정명〉 combine sounds from nature and human activities recorded in the Kensington Gardens with traditional Korean vocal music and instruments, including the *gayageum* (가야금), *geomungo* (거문고), *piri* (피리), *janggo* (장고), and *kkwaenggwari* (꽹과리).

As a response to the tradition of reciting poetry in traditional pavilions in Korea, the vocals from the two soundscapes feature lyrics borrowed from classical poems:

The Willow Is 〈버들은〉

The willow as thread,
the oriole as shuttle,
my sorrow, I wove through all ninety
    days of Spring, and still
So who can tell me
the season leaves beauty, a fragrant
    forest of green?

버들은 실이 되고
꾀꼬리는 북이 되어
구십삼춘에 짜내느니 나의 시름
누구서
녹음방초를 승화시라 하든고

Moonlight 〈월정명〉

How bright the midnight moon as
    I row on the autumn river
The sky flows in the water, the moon
    glows in the sky's centre
Child, ladle out the moon so we may
    savour it fully, and for long

월정명 월정명커늘 물을 저어 추강에 나니
물 아래 하늘이요 하늘 가운데 명월이라
선동아 잠긴 달 건저라 완월하게

The Willow Is 〈버들은〉 is presented between June and August during the summer and transitions to *Moonlight* 〈월정명〉 in September to mark the beginning of autumn.

You can listen to *The Willow Is* 〈버들은〉 and *Moonlight* 〈월정명〉 by scanning the QR code below.

Composed by Jang Young-Gyu
All instruments played by Jang Young-Gyu
Vocals by Park Minhee

This catalogue is published to accompany the Serpentine Pavilion 2024 *Archipelagic Void* designed by Minsuk Cho, Mass Studies, 7 June–27 October 2024

Serpentine Pavilion 2024
© Minsuk Cho, Mass Studies

Edited by Alexa Chow, Gonzalo Herrero Delicado and Yesomi Umolu
Copyedited by Melissa Larner
Translation from Korean by Emily Jungmin Yoon
Designed by Sulki & Min
Printed by Gomer Press in Wales, UK

First published in 2024 by Serpentine and Verlag der Buchhandlung Walther und Franz König, Köln

© 2024 Minsuk Cho, Mass Studies; Serpentine, London; the authors; and Verlag der Buchhandlung Walther und Franz König, Köln

All rights reserved. No part of this publication may be reproduced, stored in a retrieval system or transmitted in any form or by any means, electronic, mechanical, photocopying, recording or otherwise without prior permission of the publishers. The publishers of this book are committed to respecting the intellectual property rights of others. Every effort has been made to trace copyright holders and to obtain their permission for the use of copyright material. The publishers apologise for any errors or omissions in the above list and would be grateful if notified of any corrections that should be incorporated in future reprints or editions of this book.

Published by

SERPENTINE

Serpentine
Kensington Gardens
London W2 3XA
Telephone +44 (0) 207 402 6075
Fax +44 (0) 207 402 4103
www.serpentinegalleries.org

Verlag der Buchhandlung Walther und Franz Konig
Ehrenstr. 4
D-50672 Köln

Bibliographic information published by the Deutsche Nationalbibliothek. The Deutsche National-bibliothek lists this publication in the Deutsche Nationalbibliografie; detailed bibliographic data are available on the Internet at http://dnb.d-nb.de.

Distribution

Europe
Buchhandlung Walther König
Ehrenstr. 4
D-50672 Köln
Telephone +49 (0) 221 / 20 59 6 53
verlag@buchhandlung-walther-koenig.de

UK & Ireland
ART DATA
12 Bell Industrial Estate
50 Cunnington Street
London W4 5HB
United Kingdom
Telephone +44 (0)208 747 10 61
Fax +44 (0)208 742 23 19
orders@artdata.co.uk

Outside Europe
D.A.P. / Distributed Art Publishers, Inc.
75 Broad Street, Suite 630
USA – New York, NY 10004
Telephone +1 (0) 212 627 1999
orders@dapinc.com

ISBN 978-1-908617-86-6
Serpentine, London

ISBN 978-3-7533-0688-9
Verlag der Buchhandlung Walther und Franz König, Köln

Serpentine Pavilion 2024
Archipelagic Void
Mass Studies

Photo Essay

Serpentine Pavilion 2024 Archipelagic Void   **Mass Studies**

Edited by
Alexa Chow, Gonzalo Herrero Delicado
and Yesomi Umolu

Iwan Baan   **Photo Essay**

Iwan Baan is a Dutch architecture and documentary photographer based in Amsterdam. His work captures the life of architecture globally from informal and traditional housing structures to the growth of megacities, and how individuals, communities and societies reappropriate their built environment to make it their own. He has collaborated with architects like OMA/Rem Koolhaas, Herzog & de Meuron and Zaha Hadid. His photographs are regularly featured in newspapers and magazines such as *The New York Times*, *The Wall Street Journal* and *Architectural Digest*. He has contributed to books such as *Rome–Las Vegas: Bread and Circuses* (2024) and *African Modernism: The Architecture of Independence* (2015/2022). His retrospective exhibition launched at the Vitra Design Museum in 2023/2024.

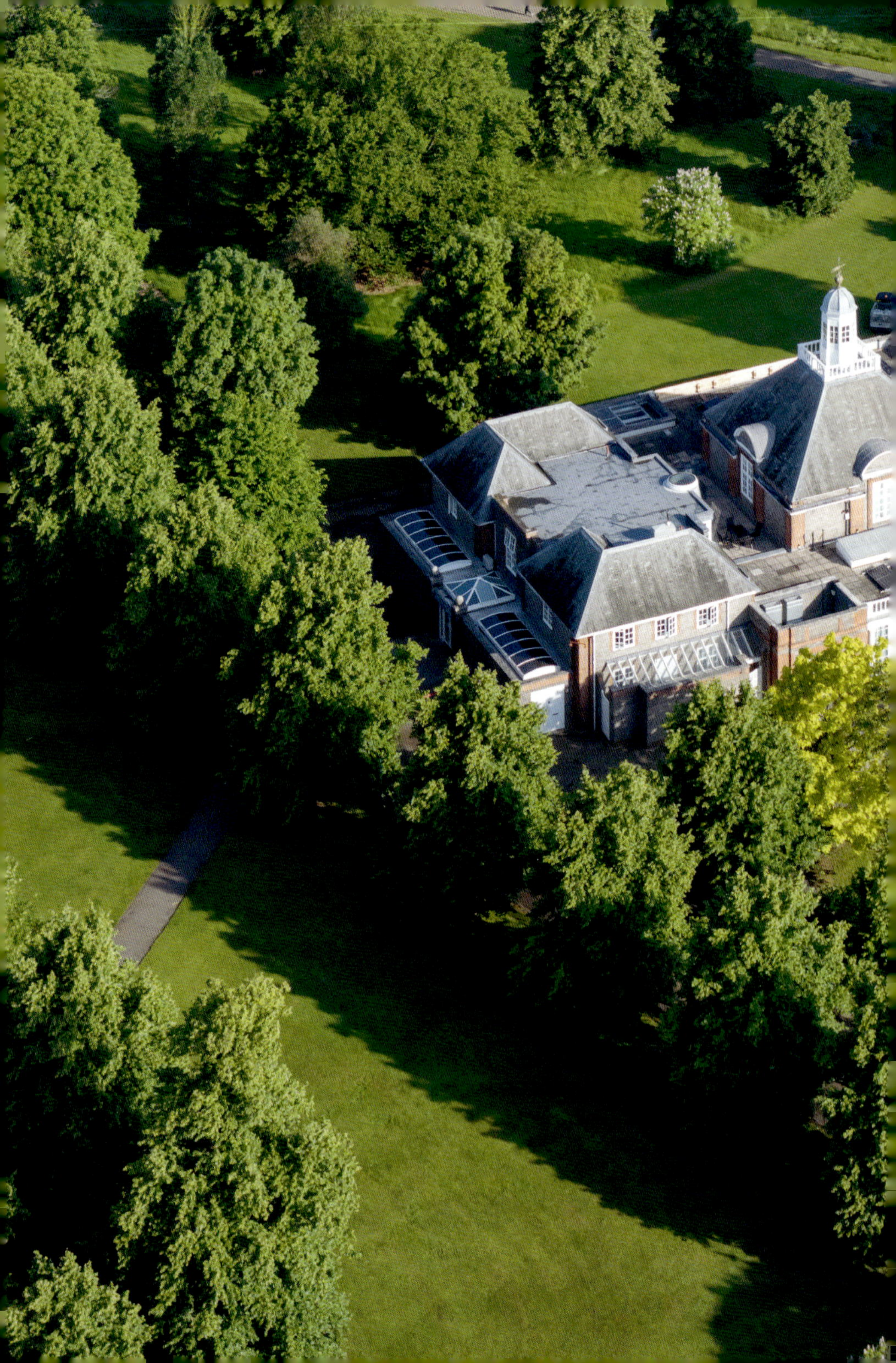

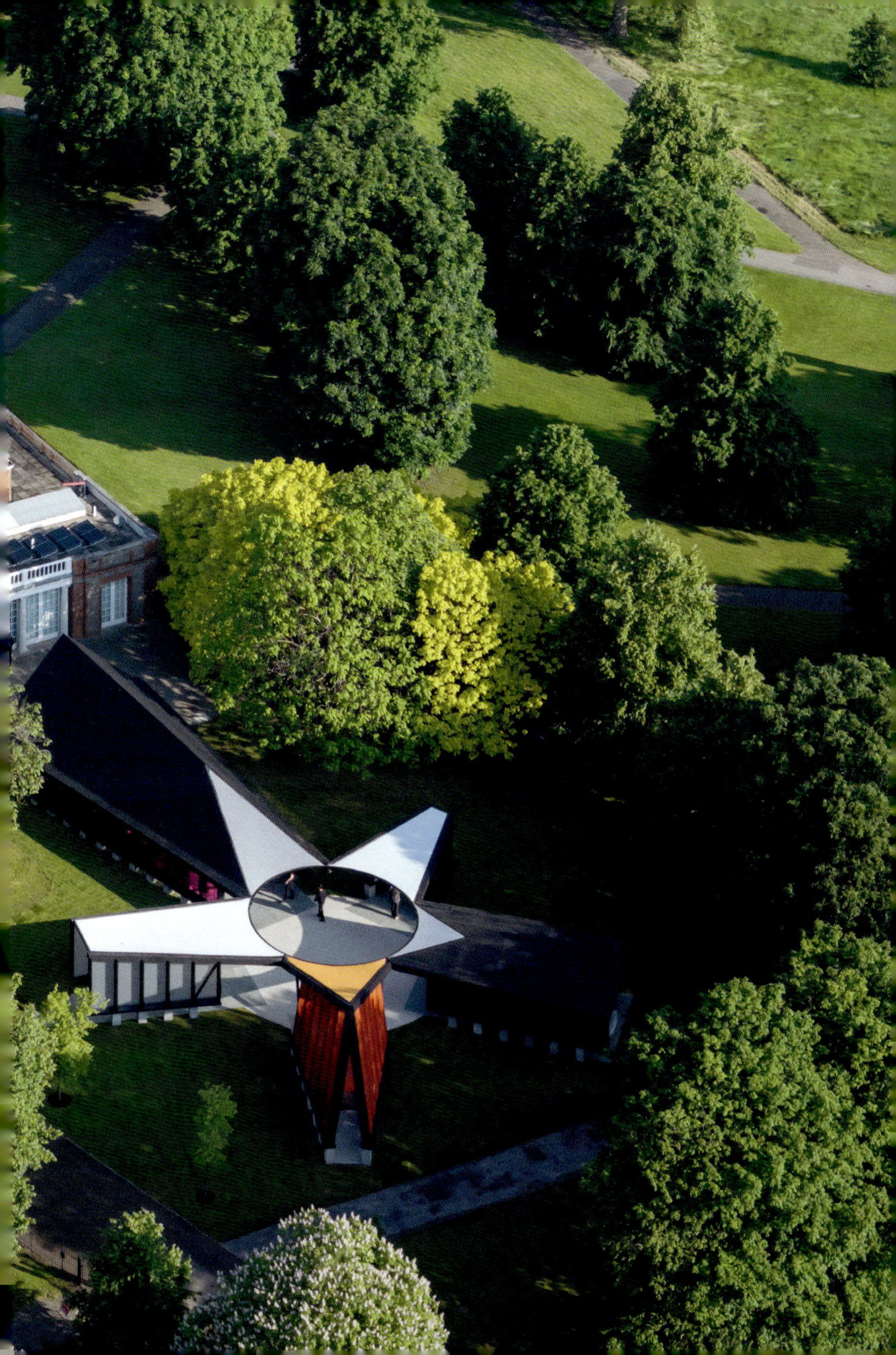

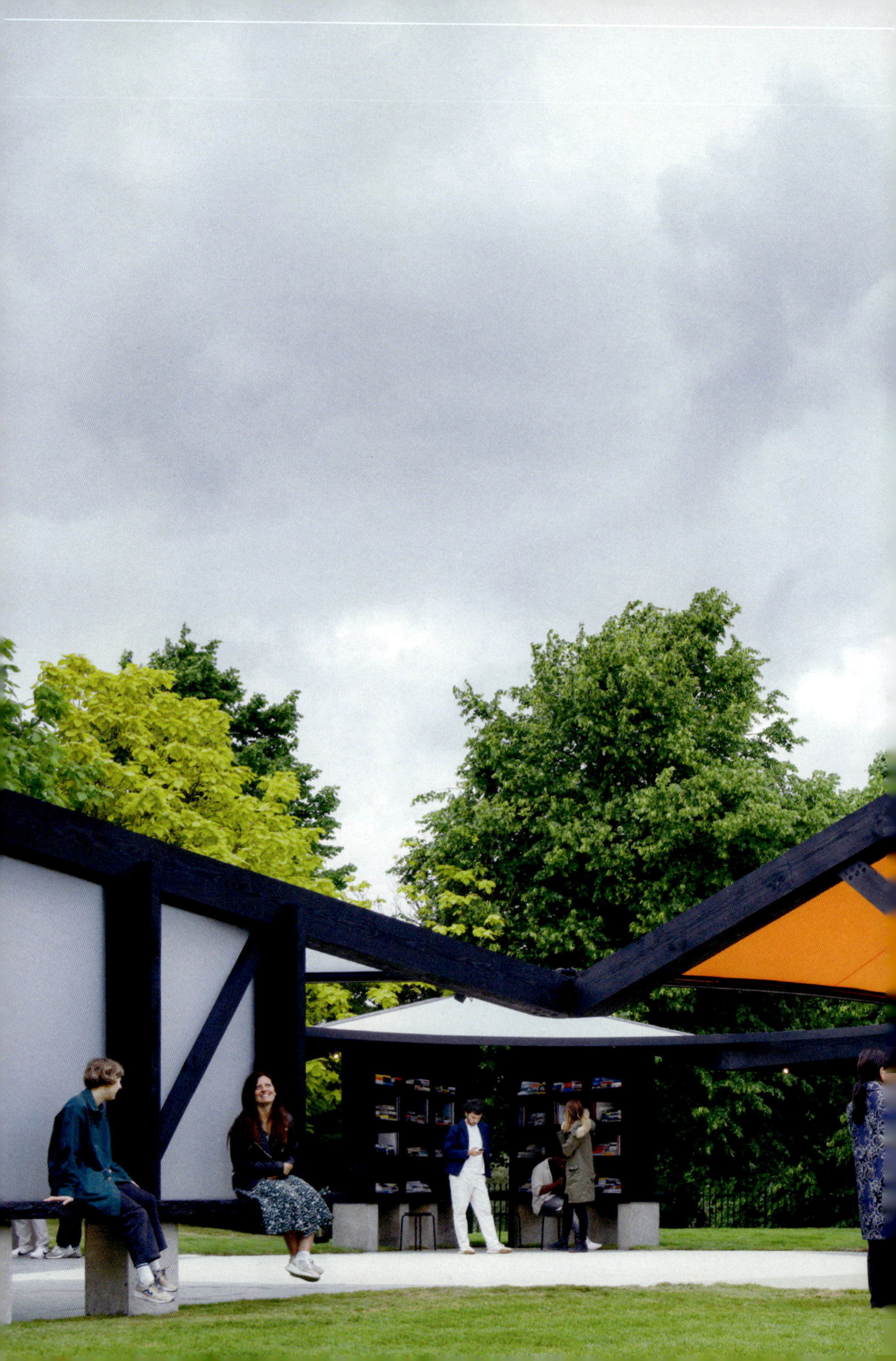

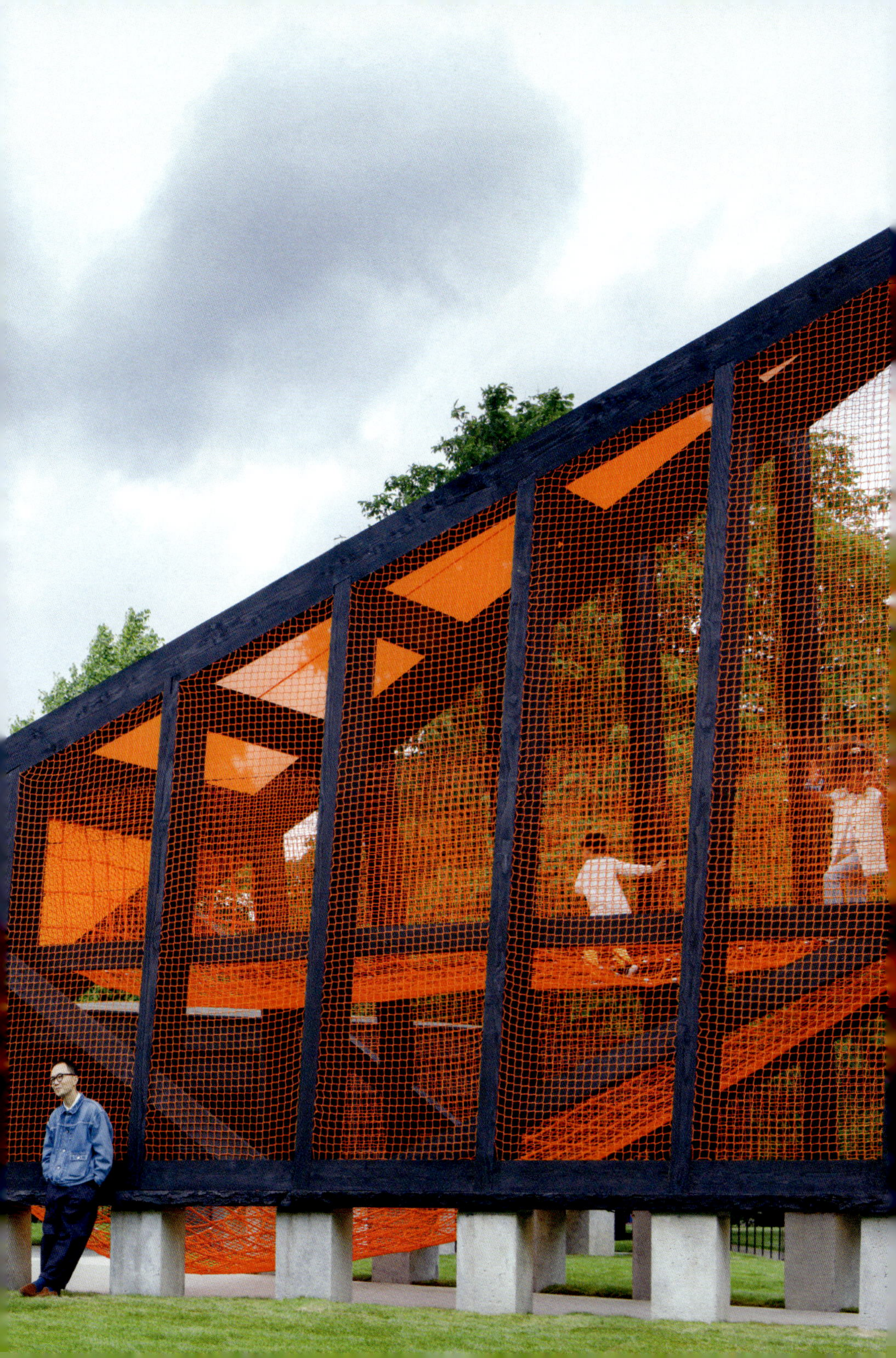

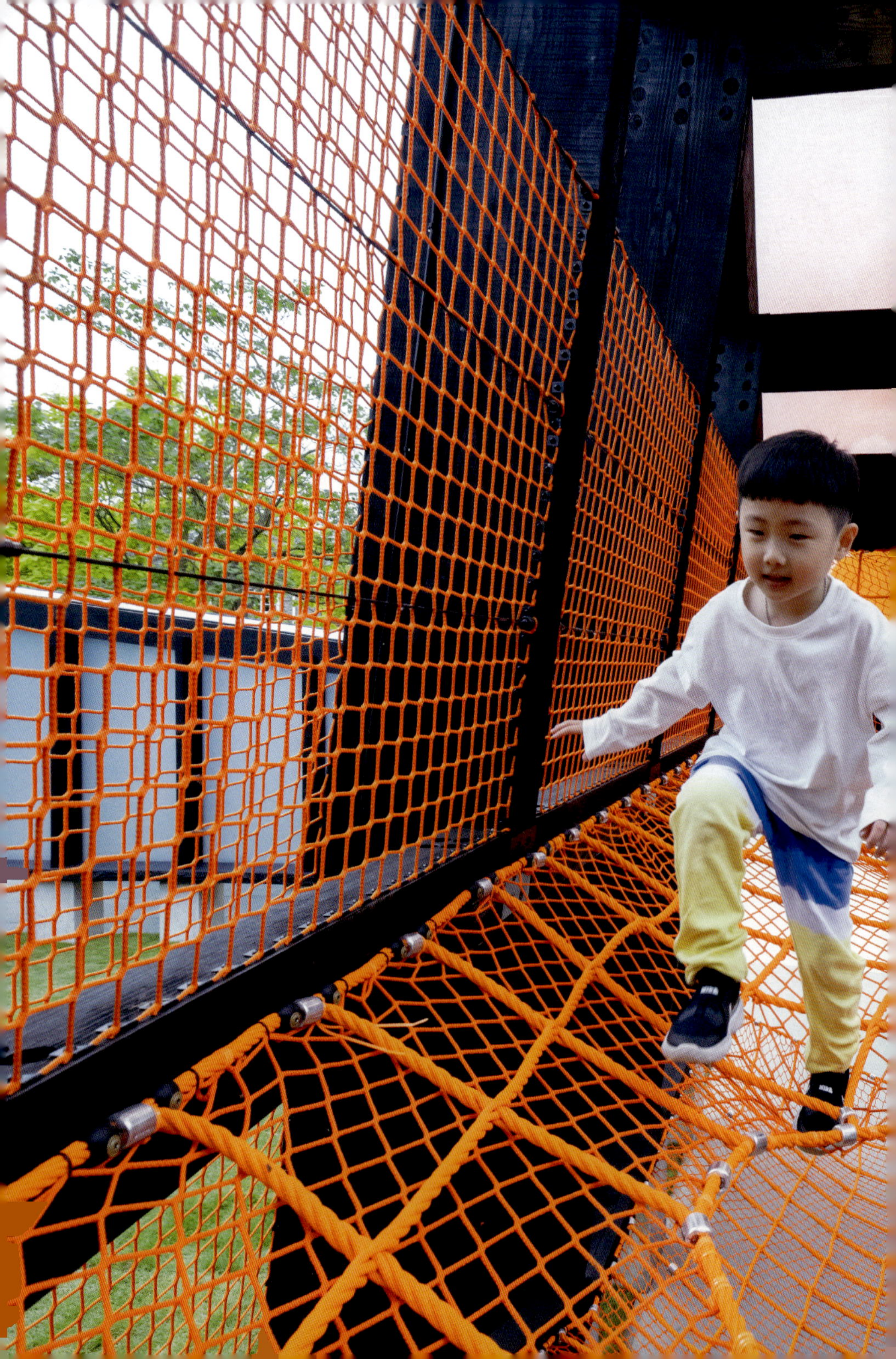

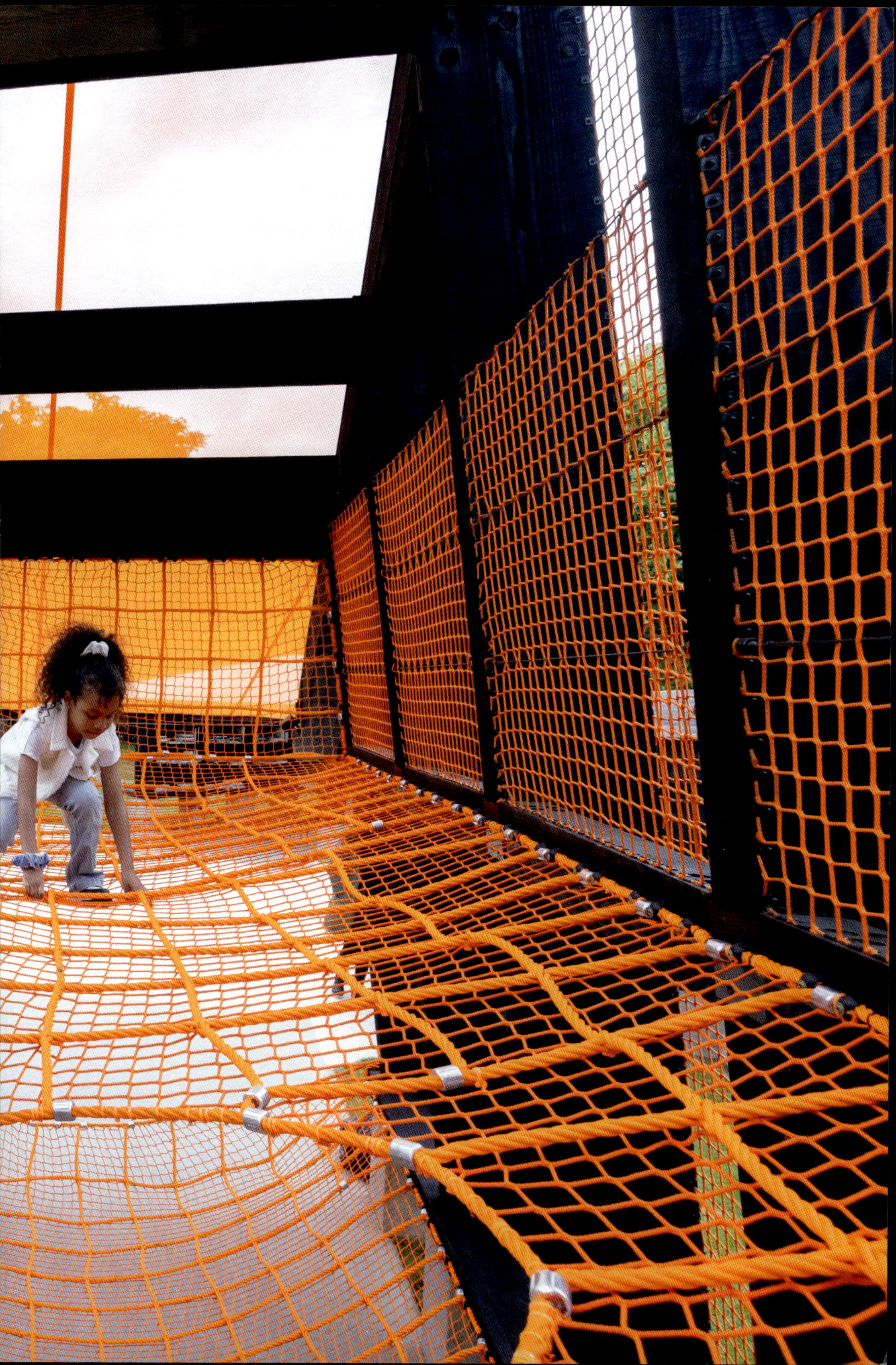

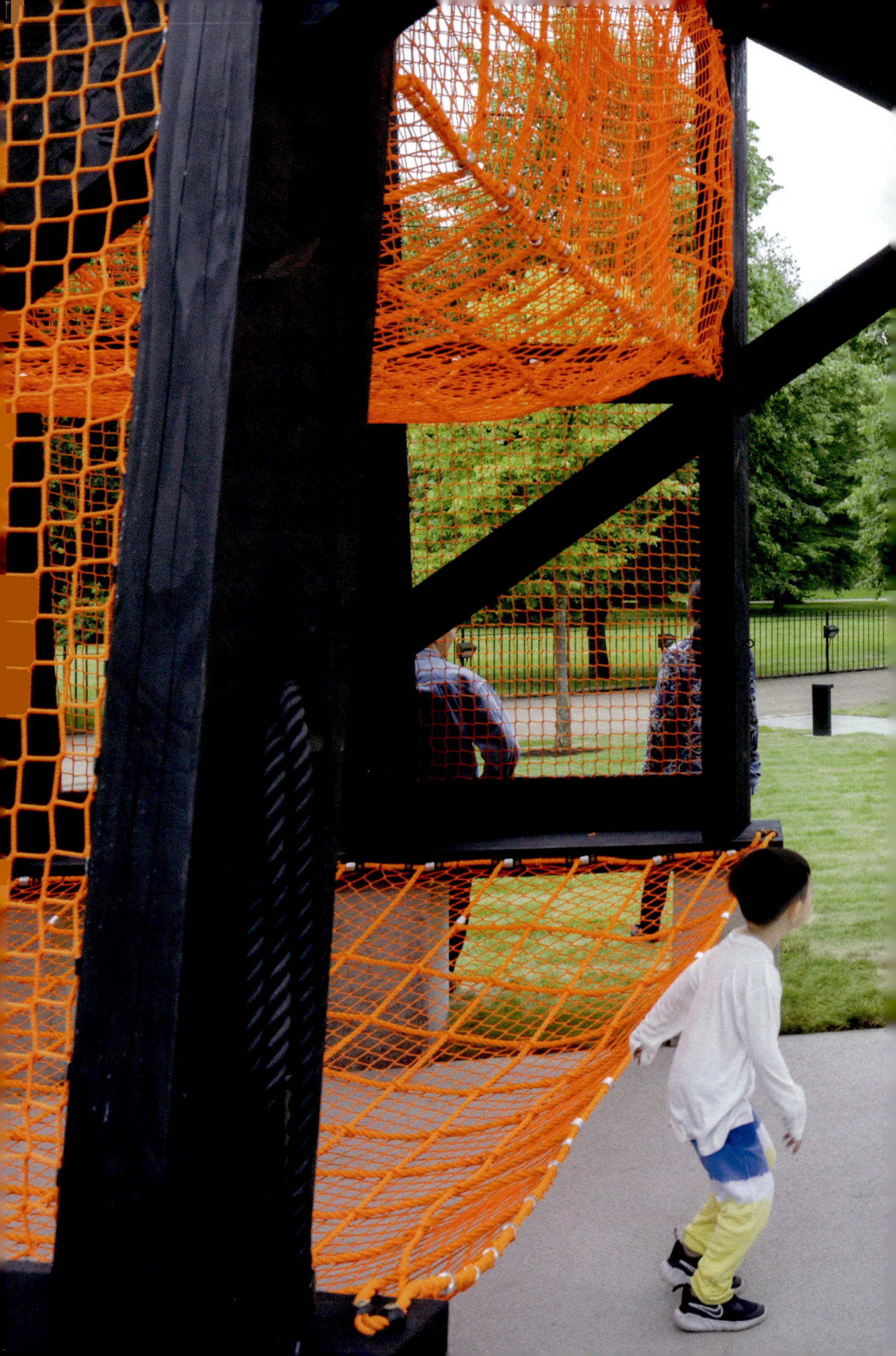

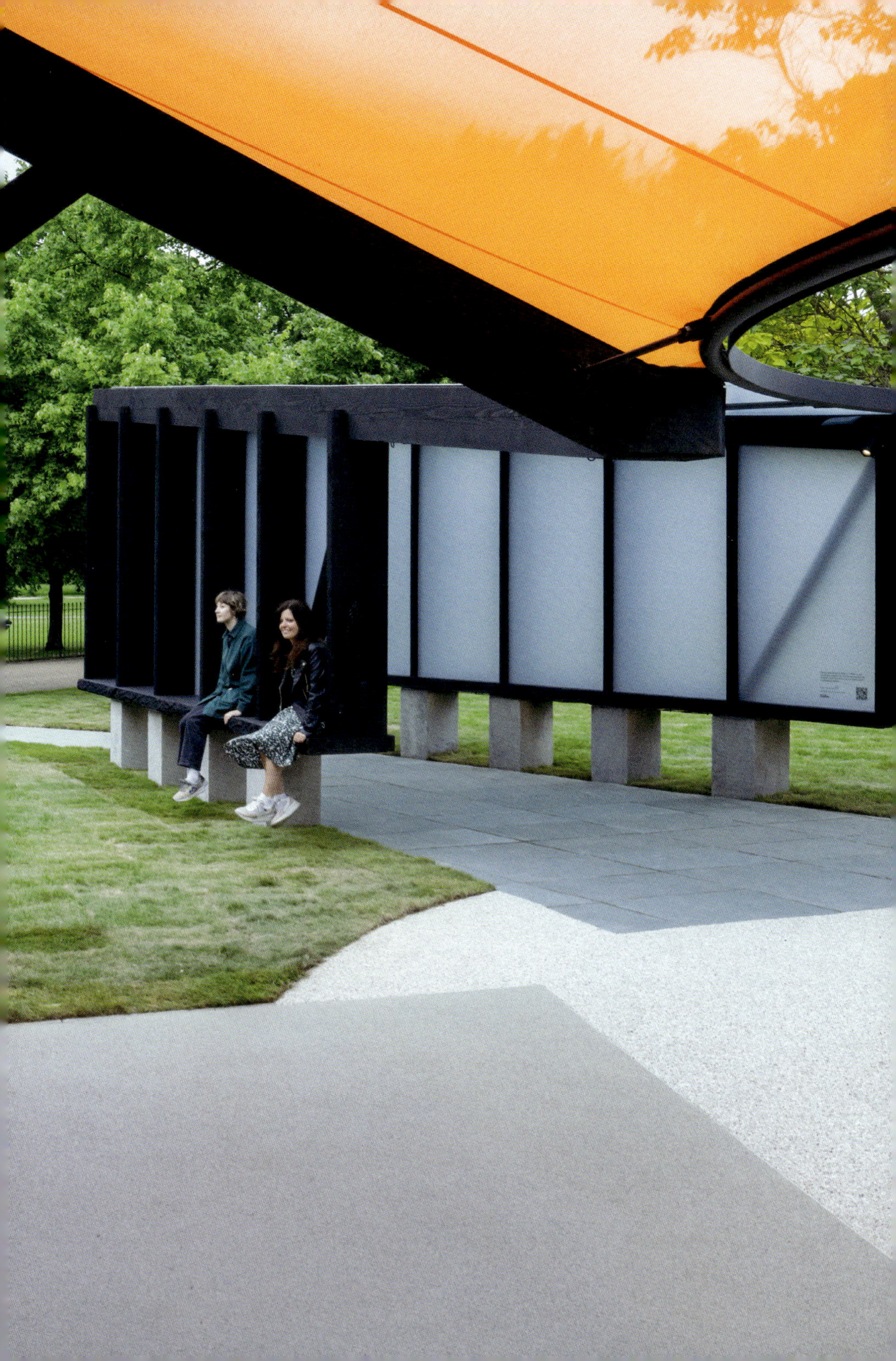

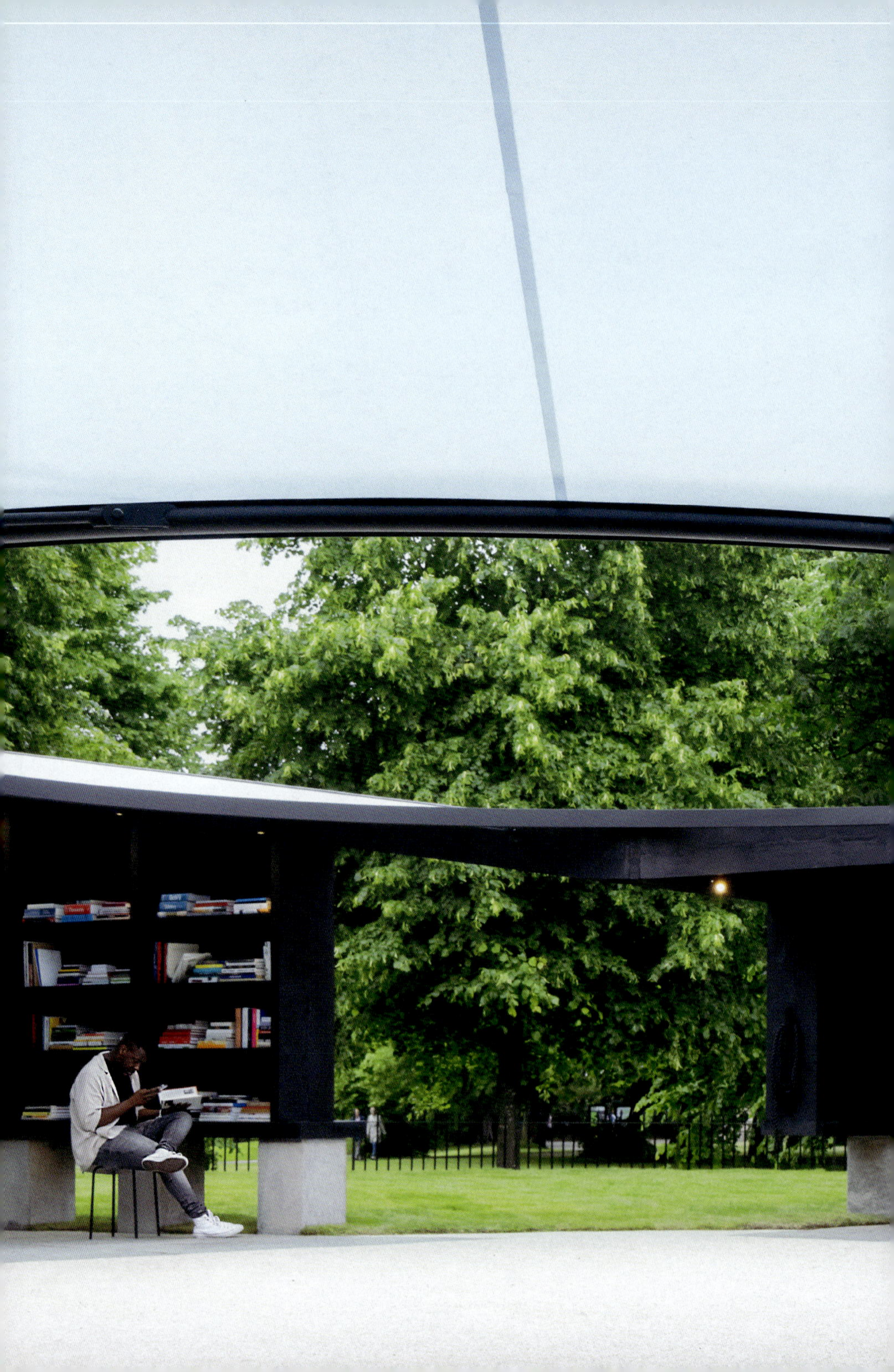

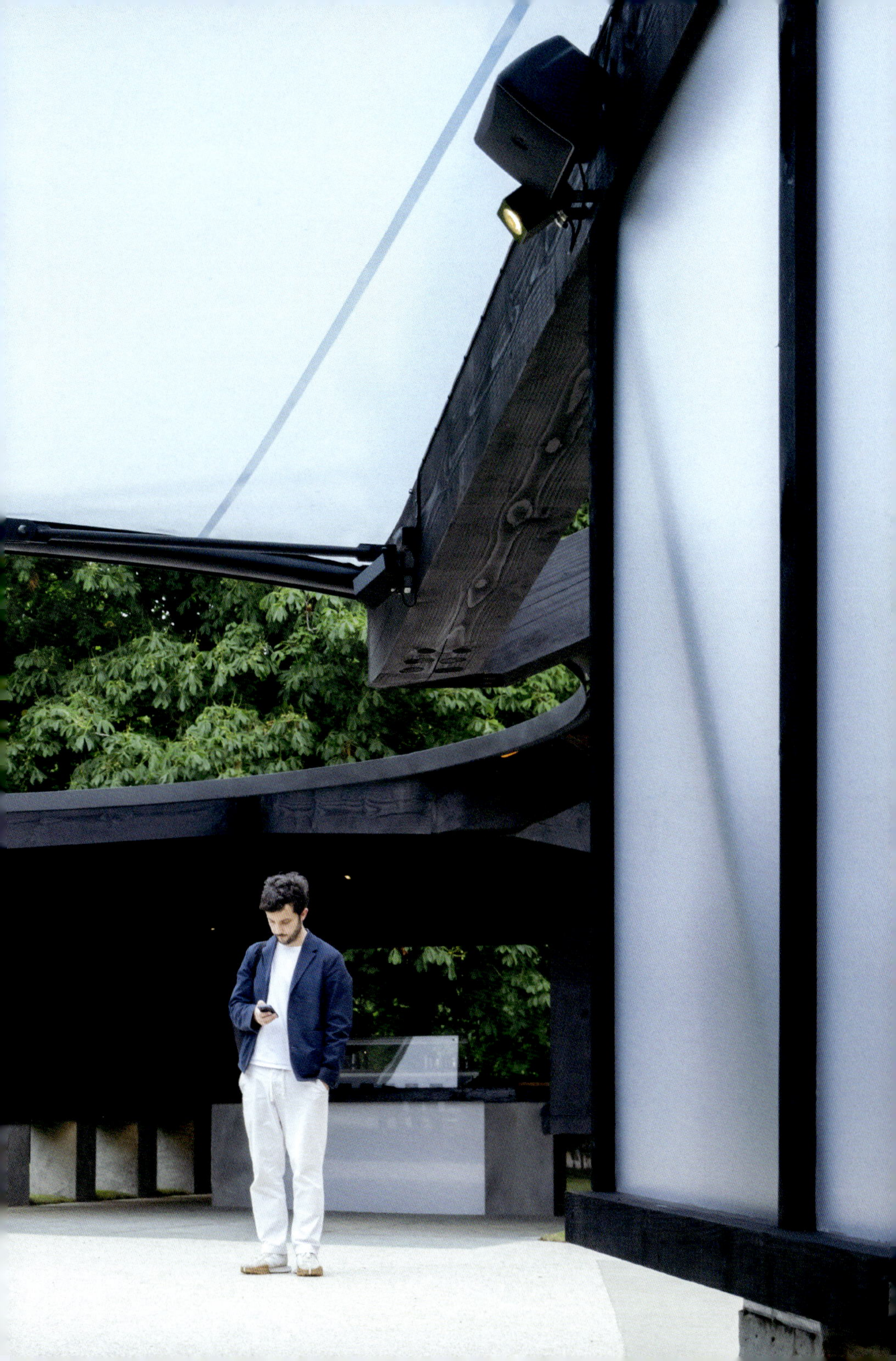

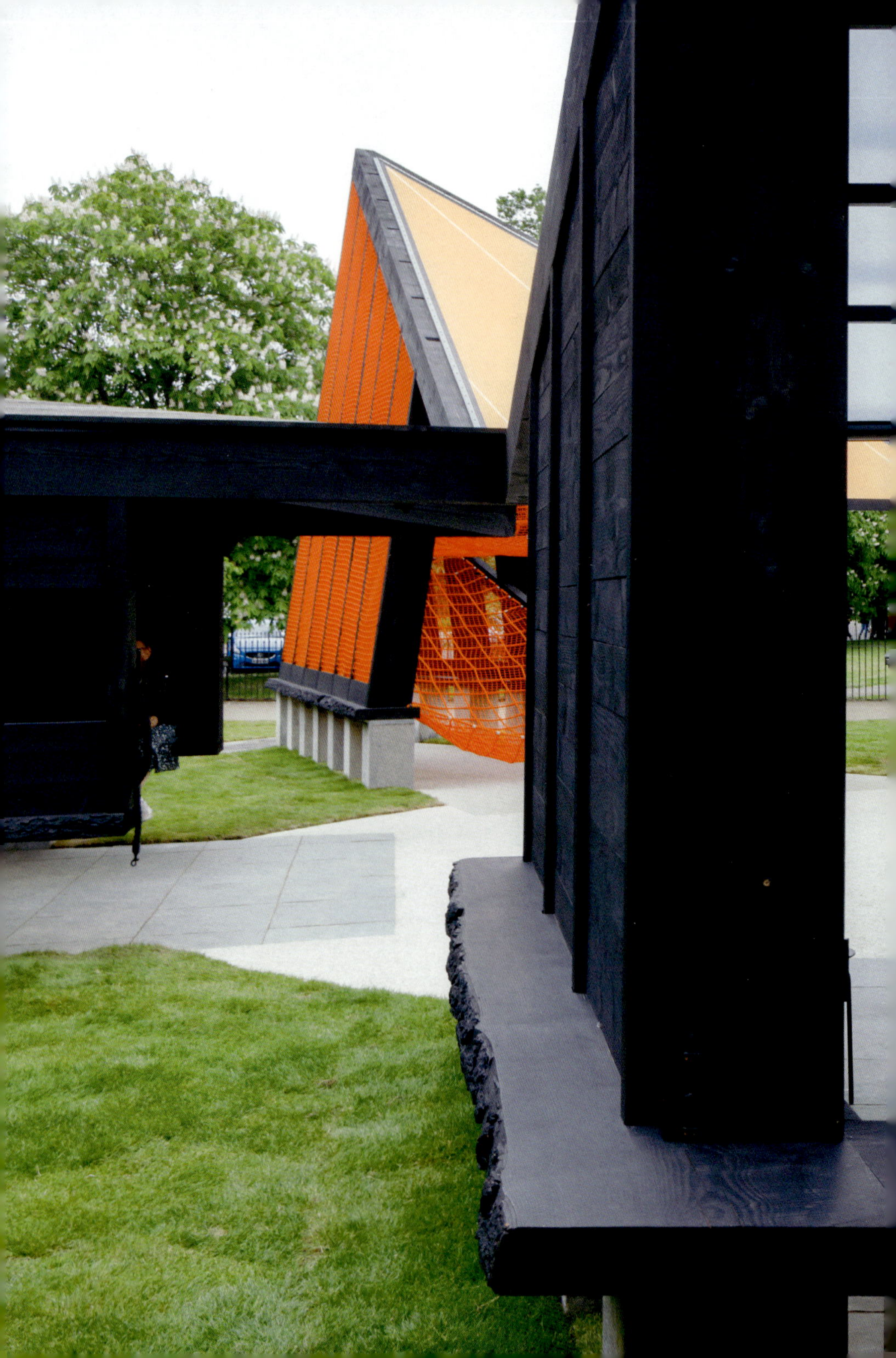

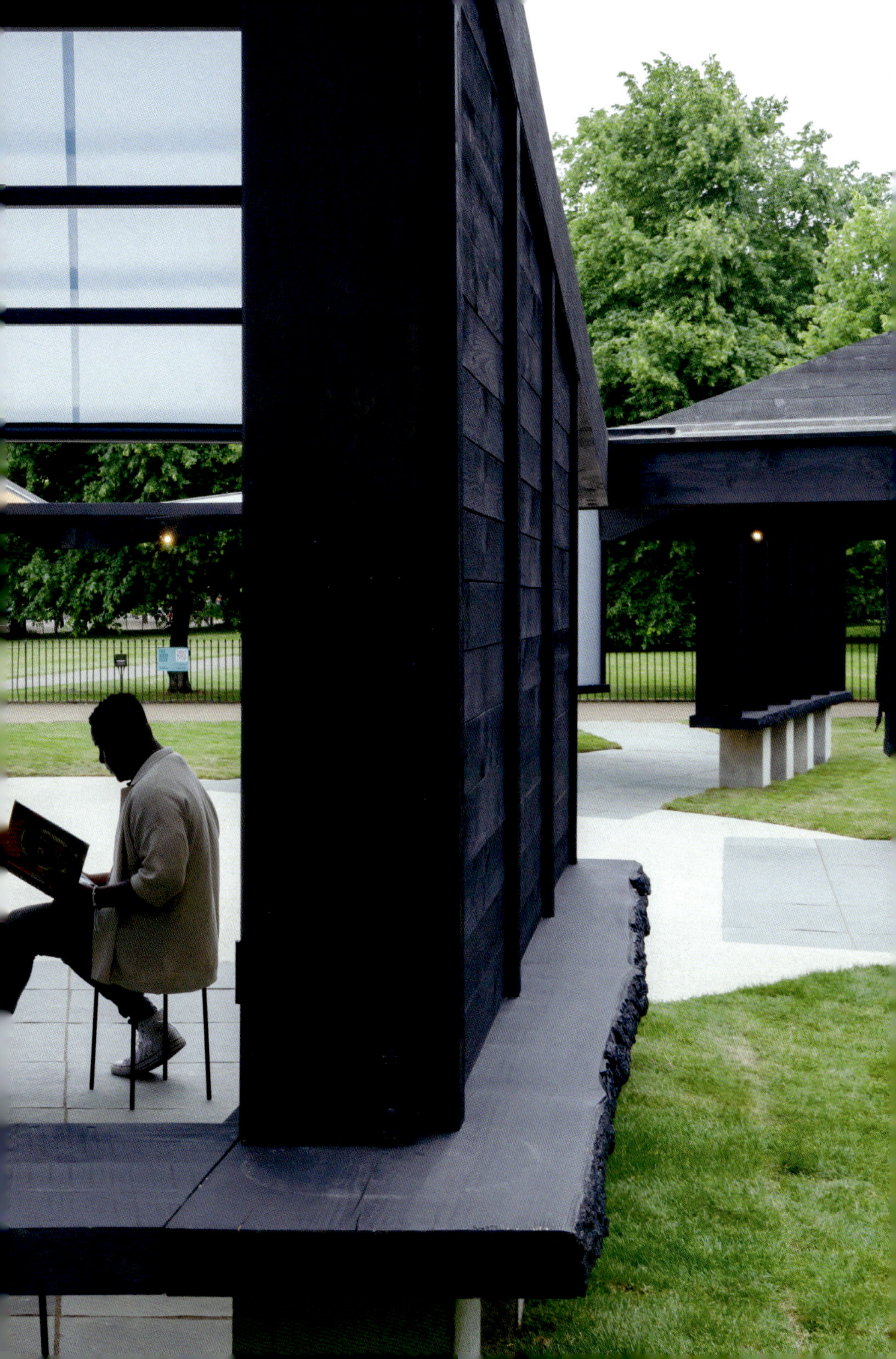

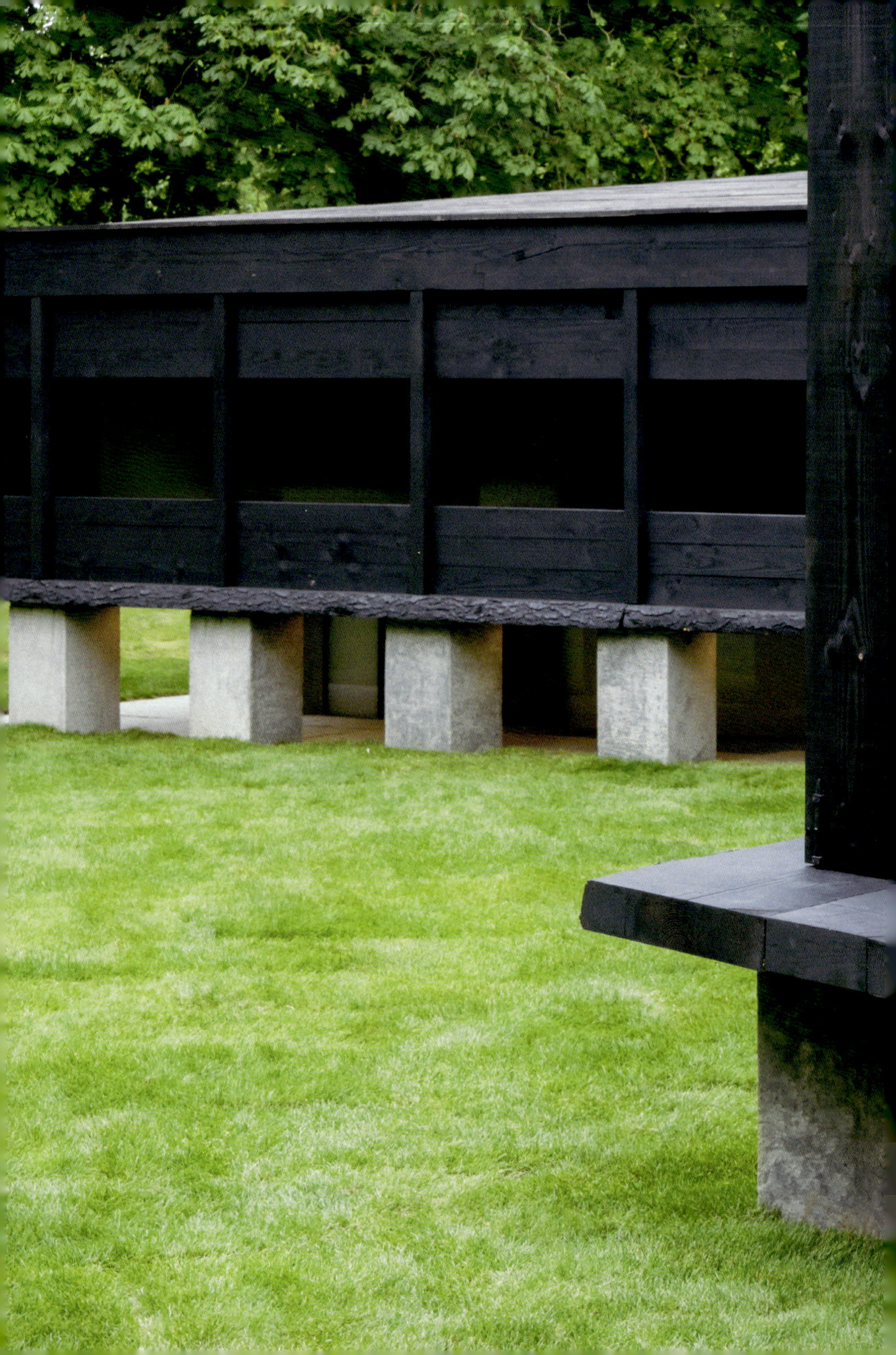

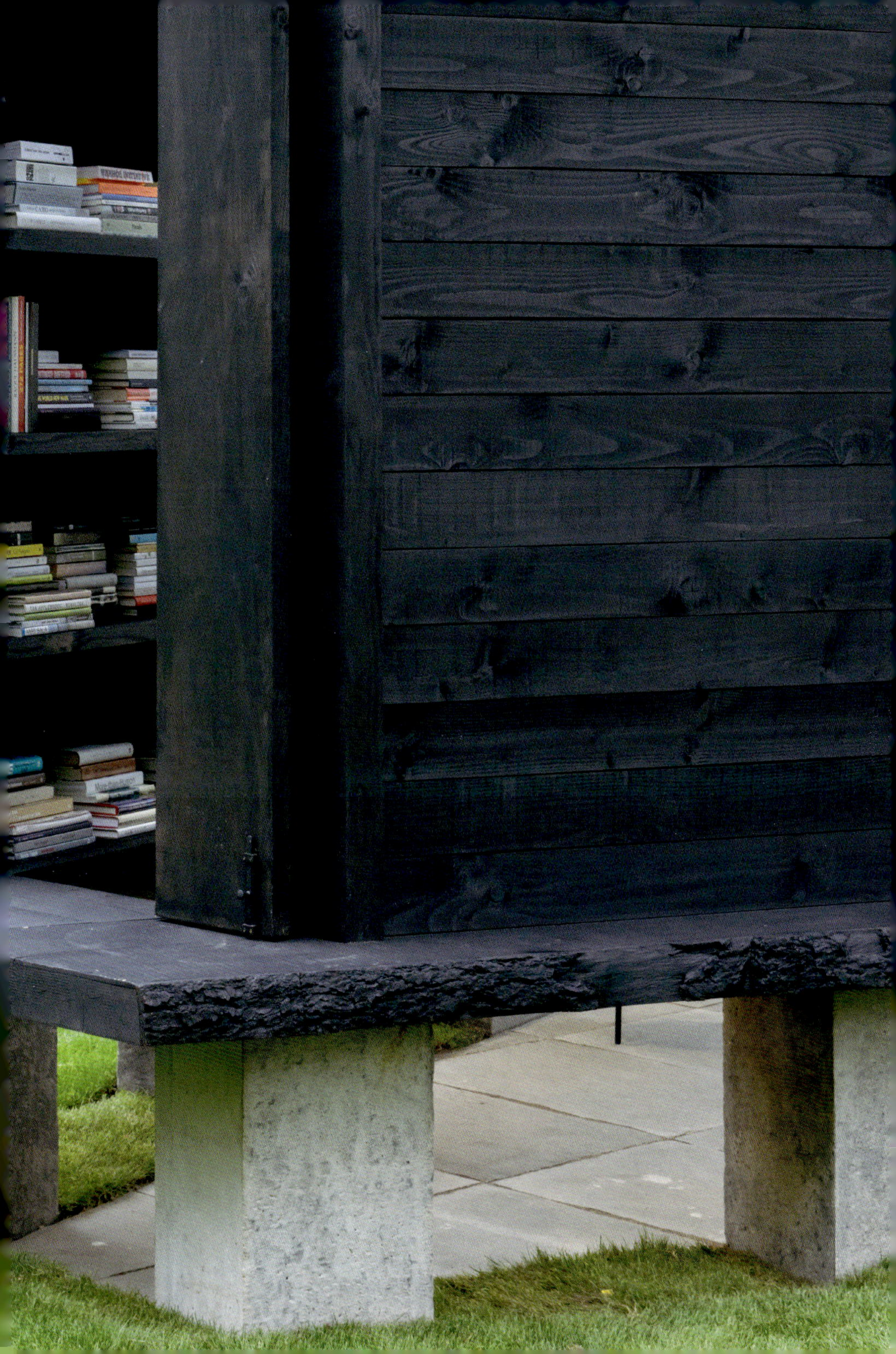

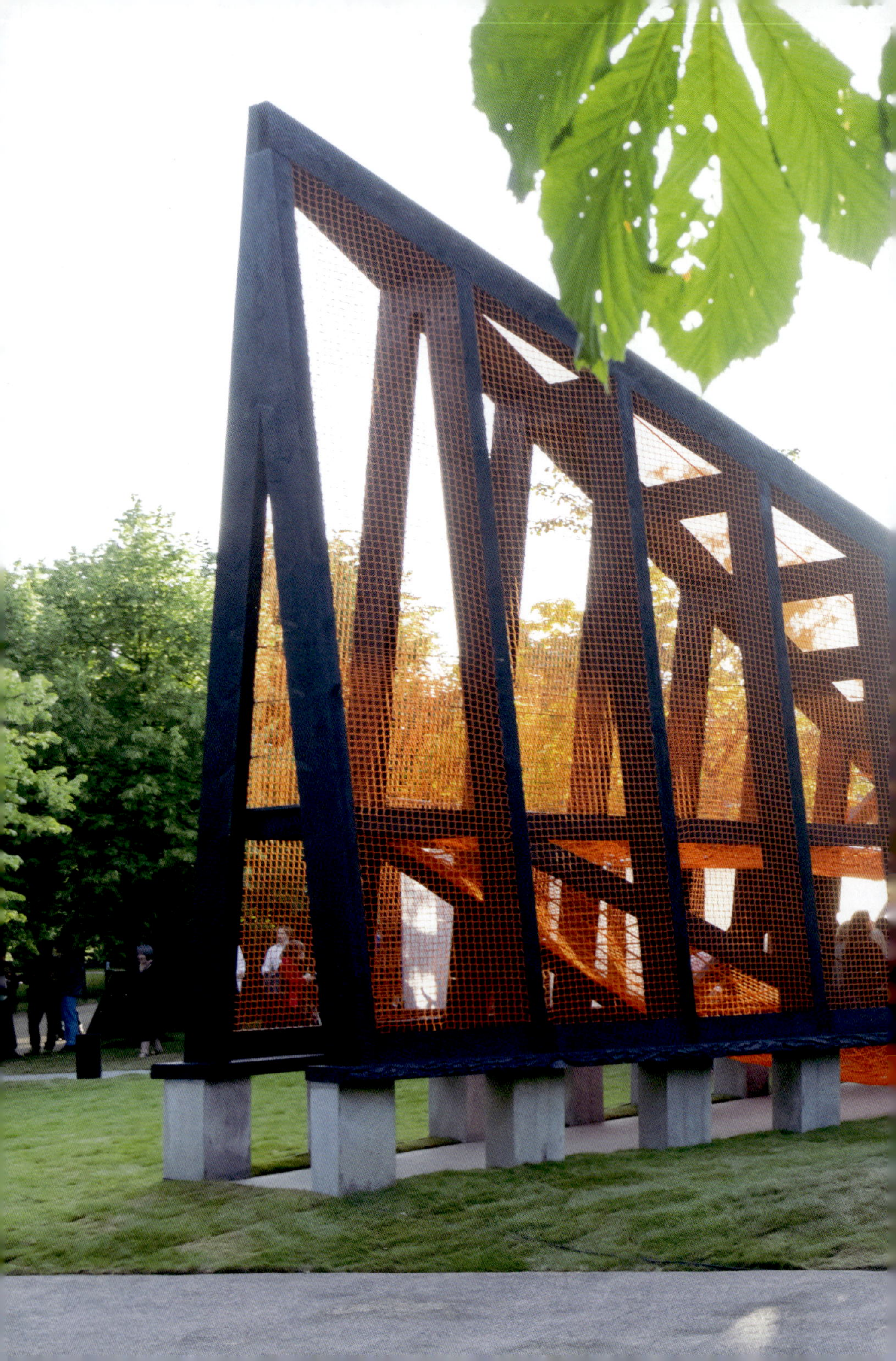

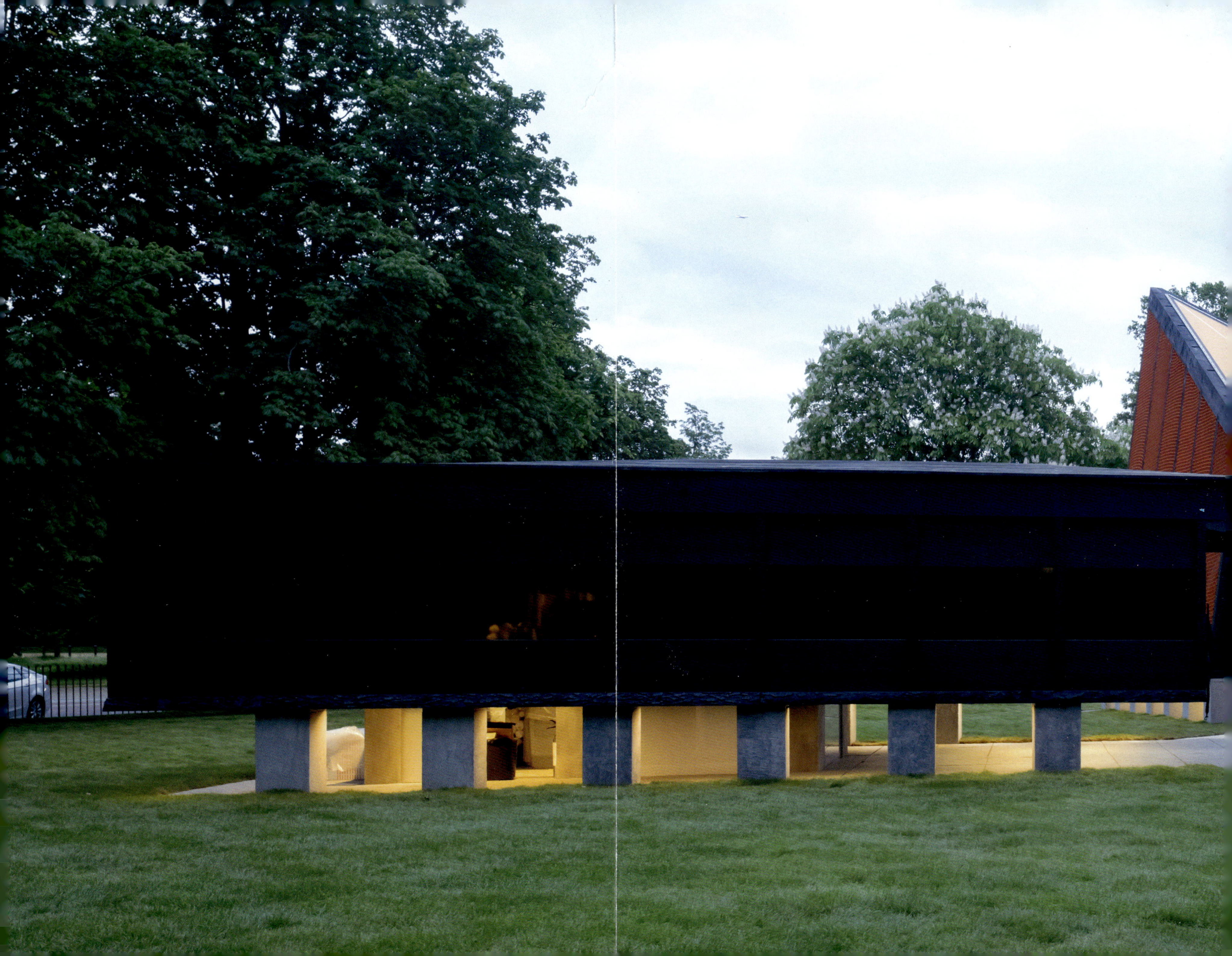

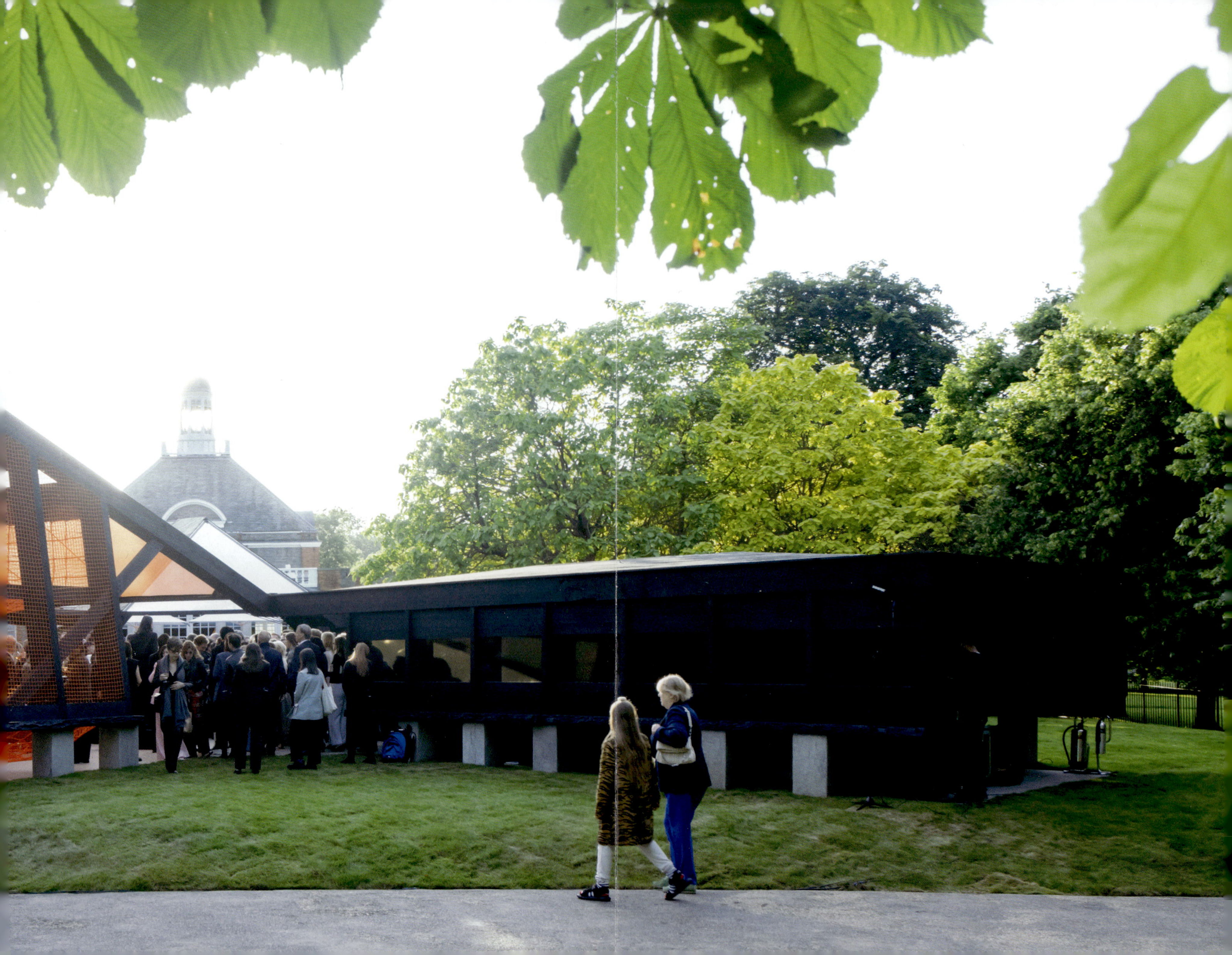

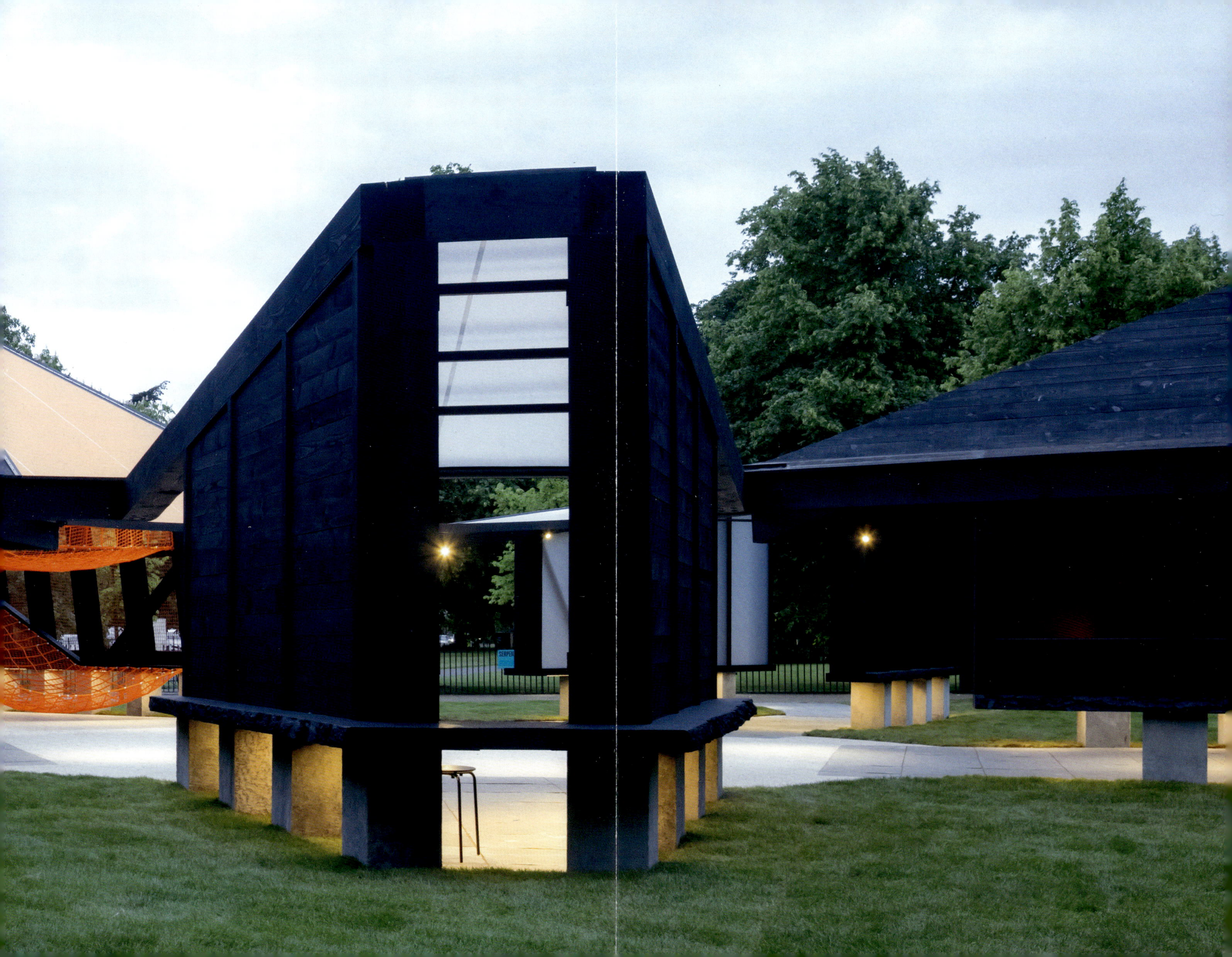

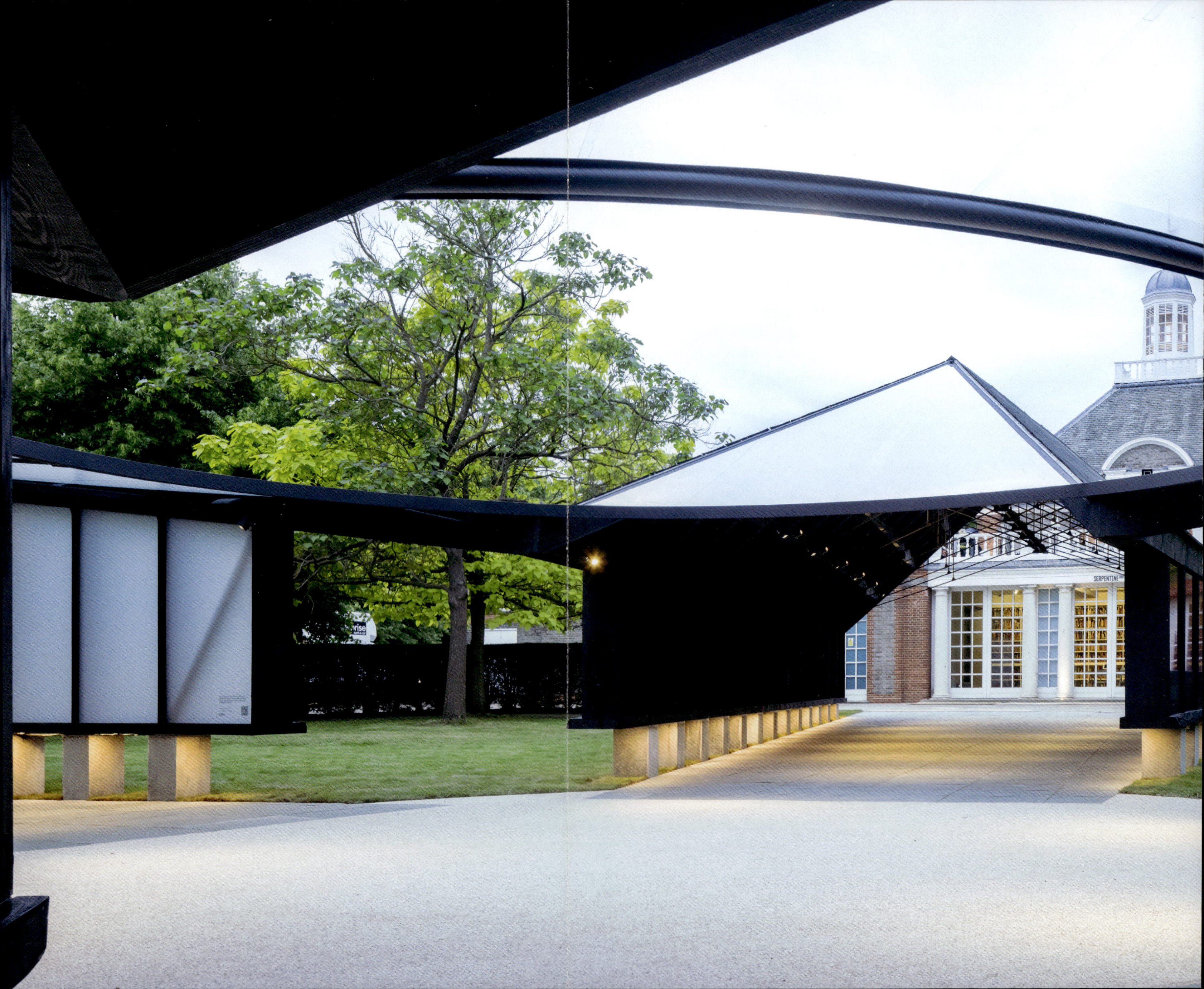
SERPENTINE

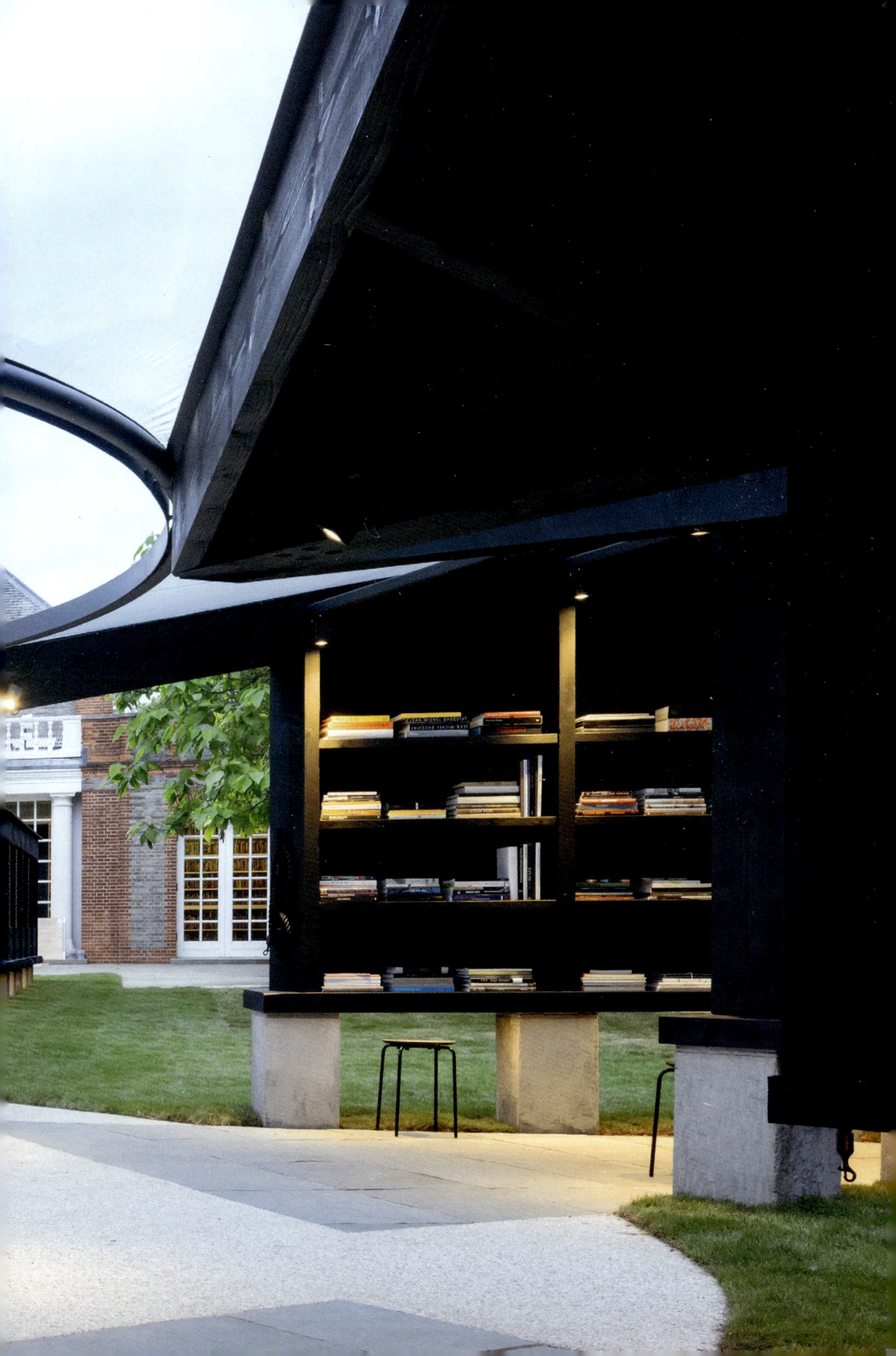

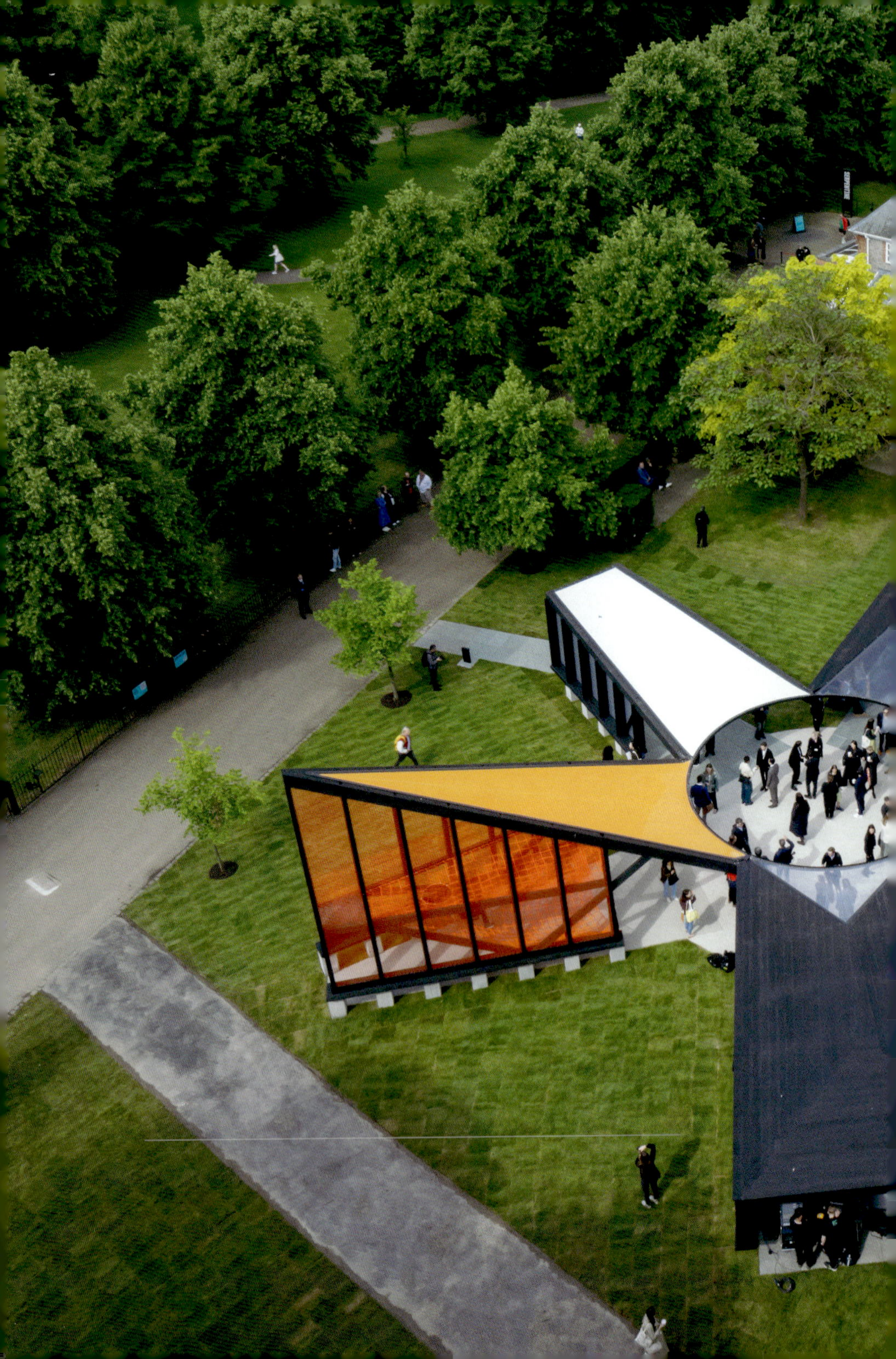

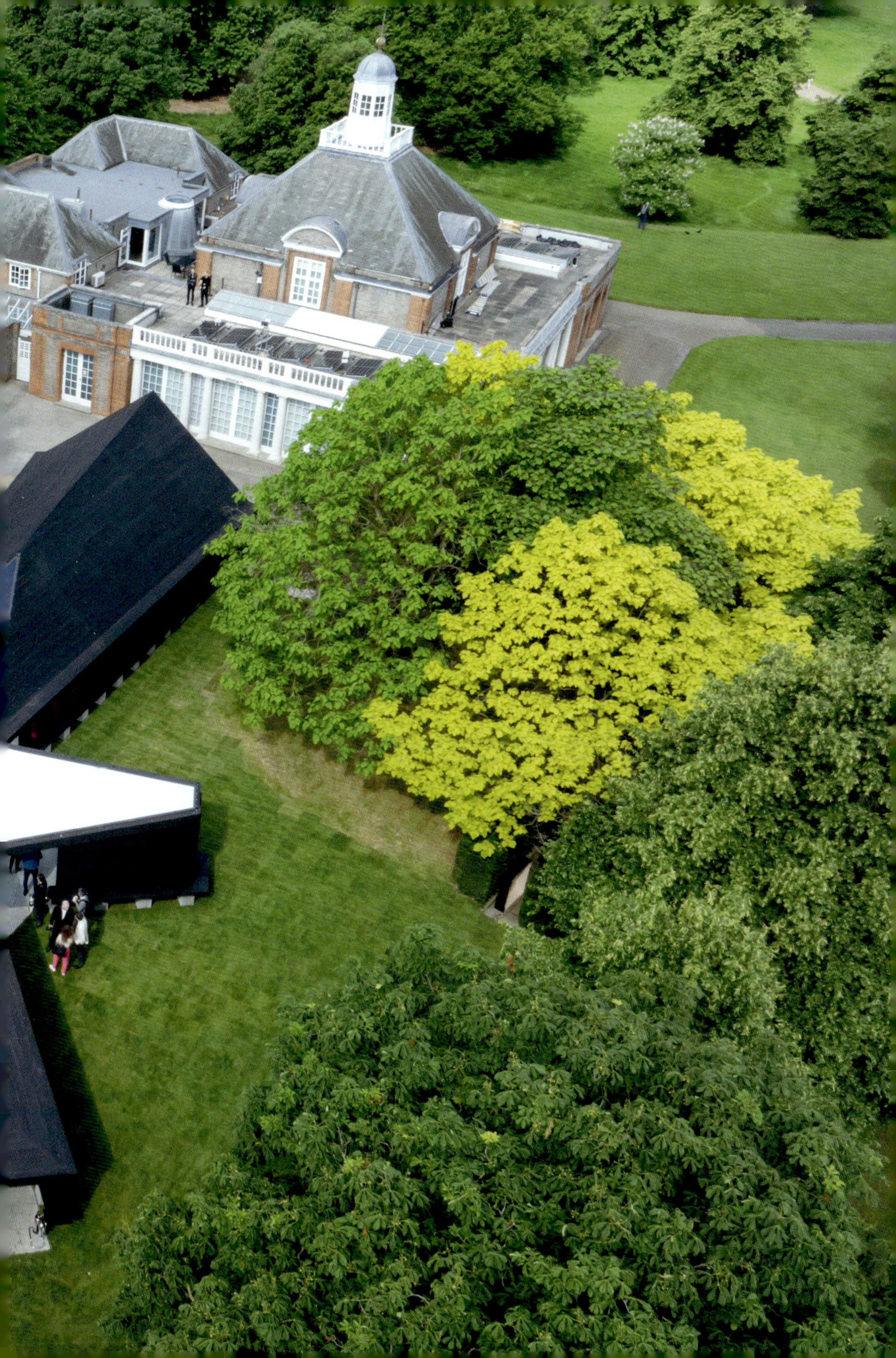

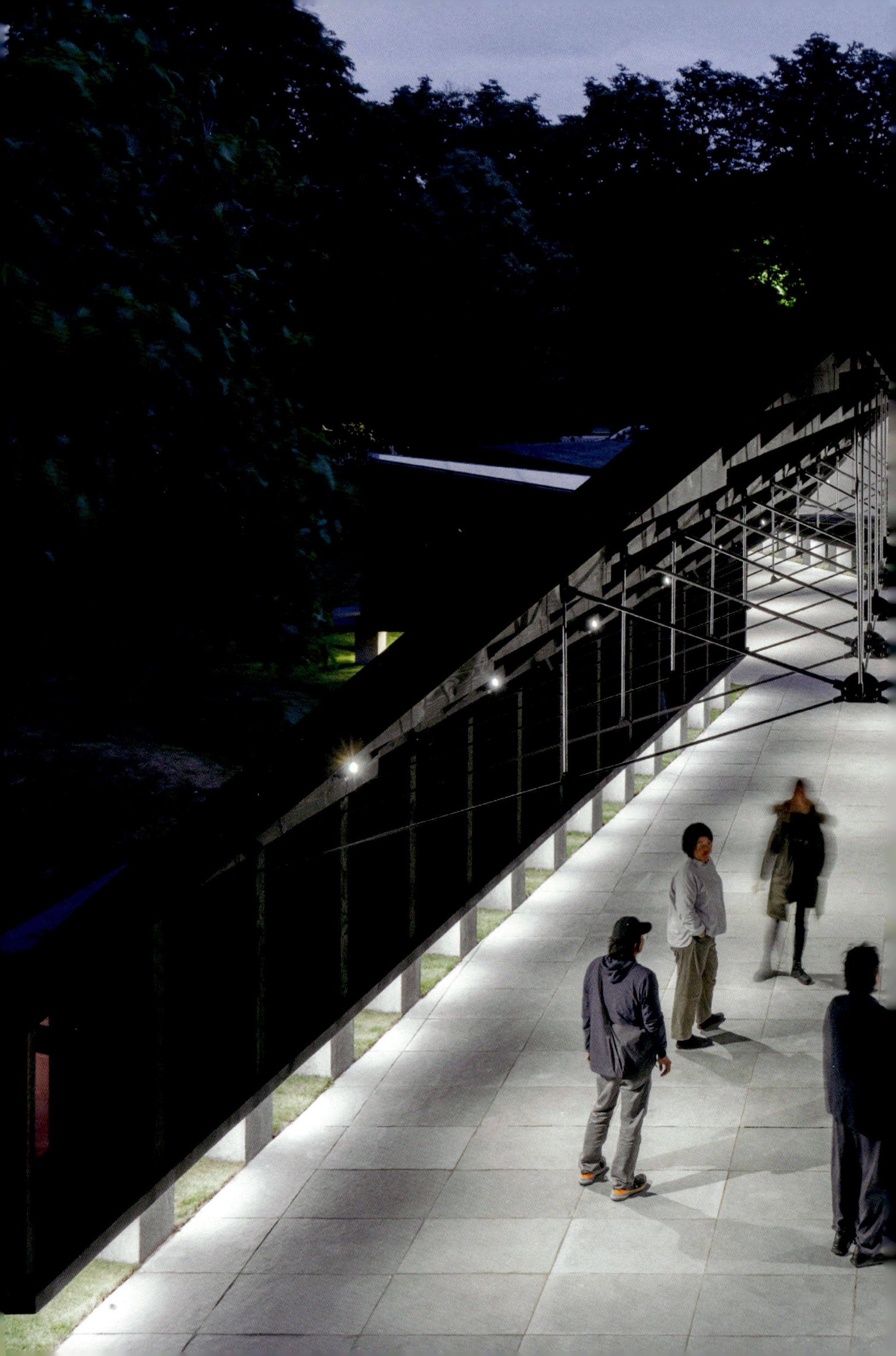

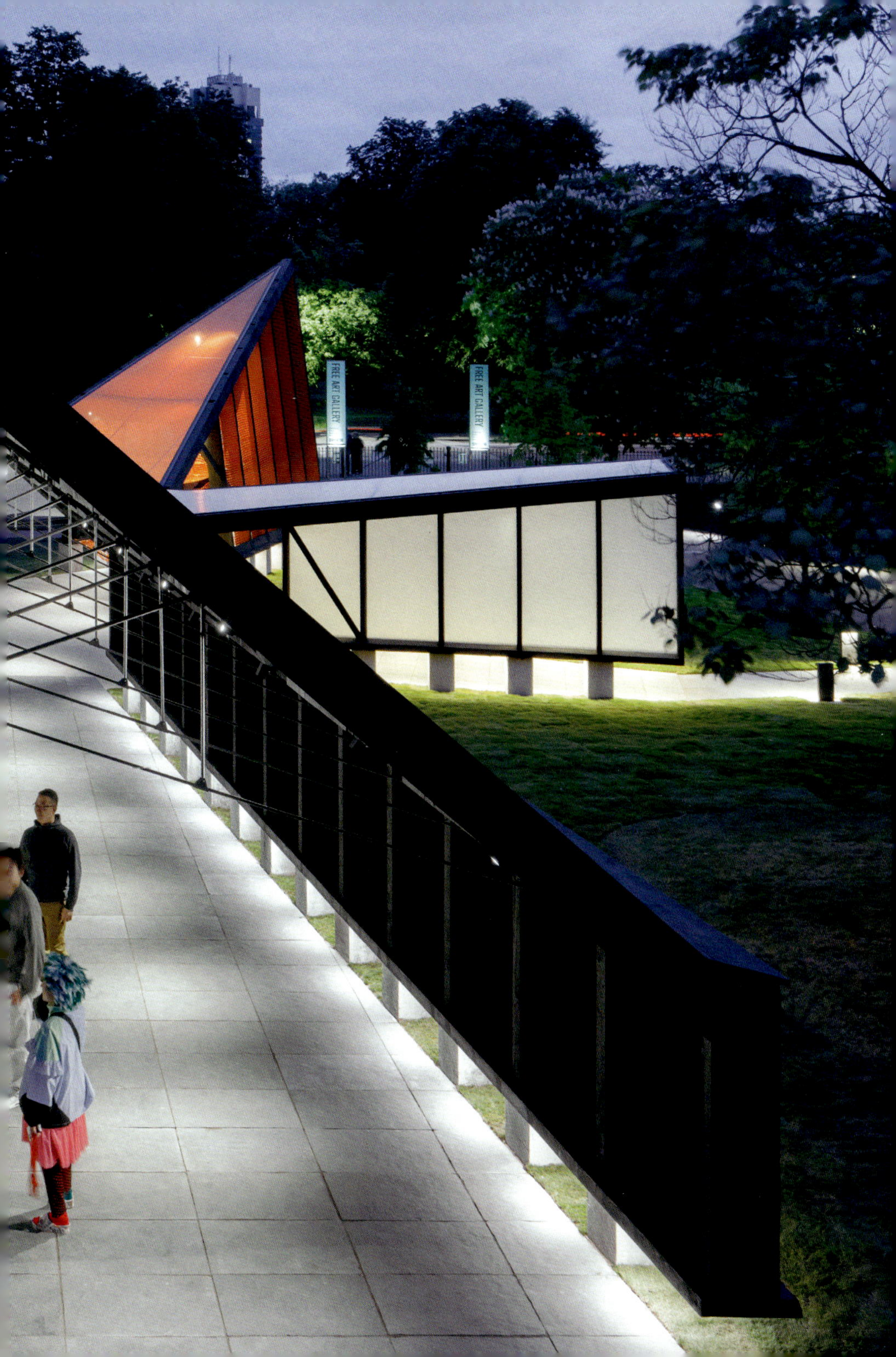
FREE ART GALLERY
FREE ART GALLERY

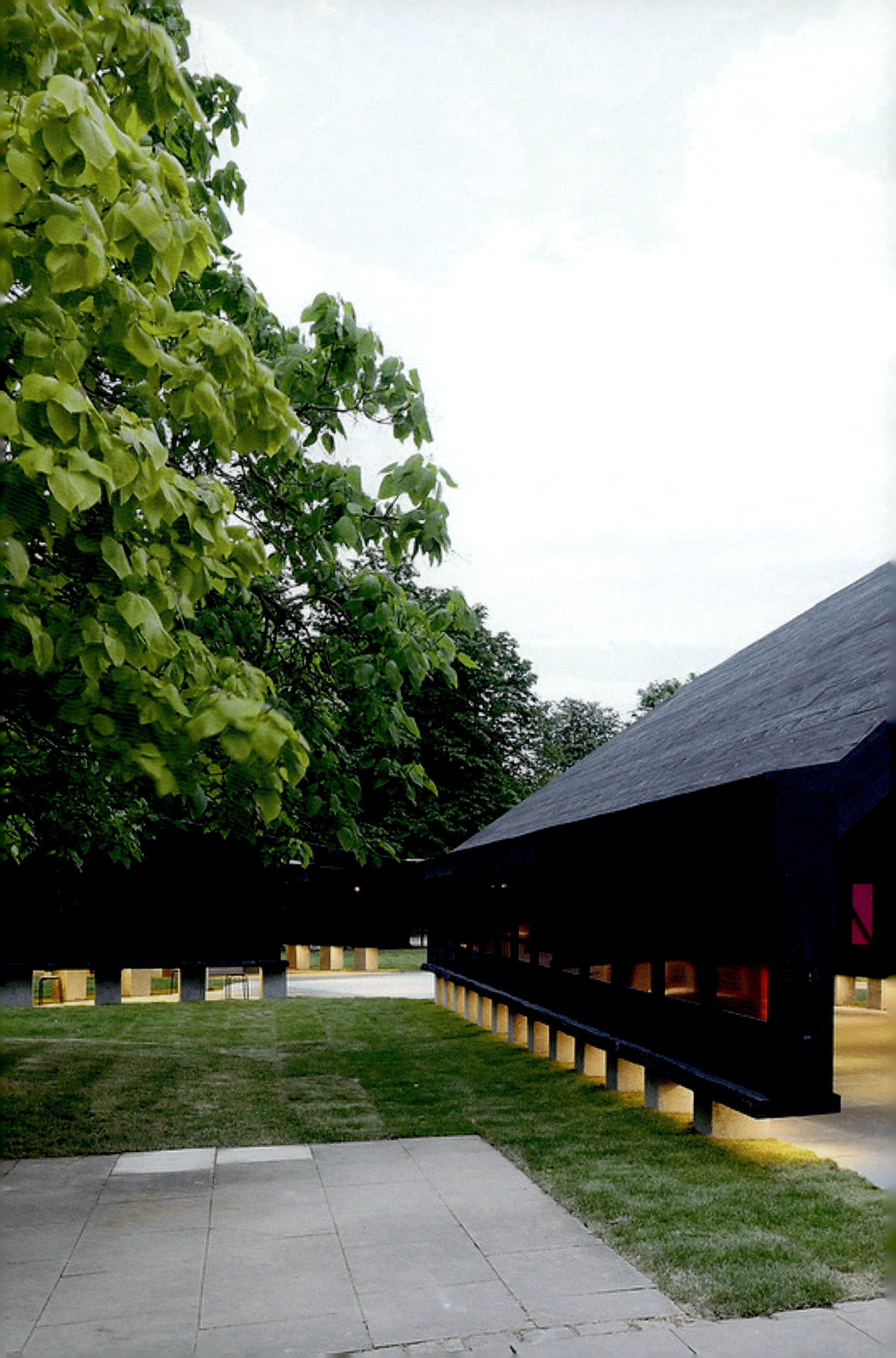

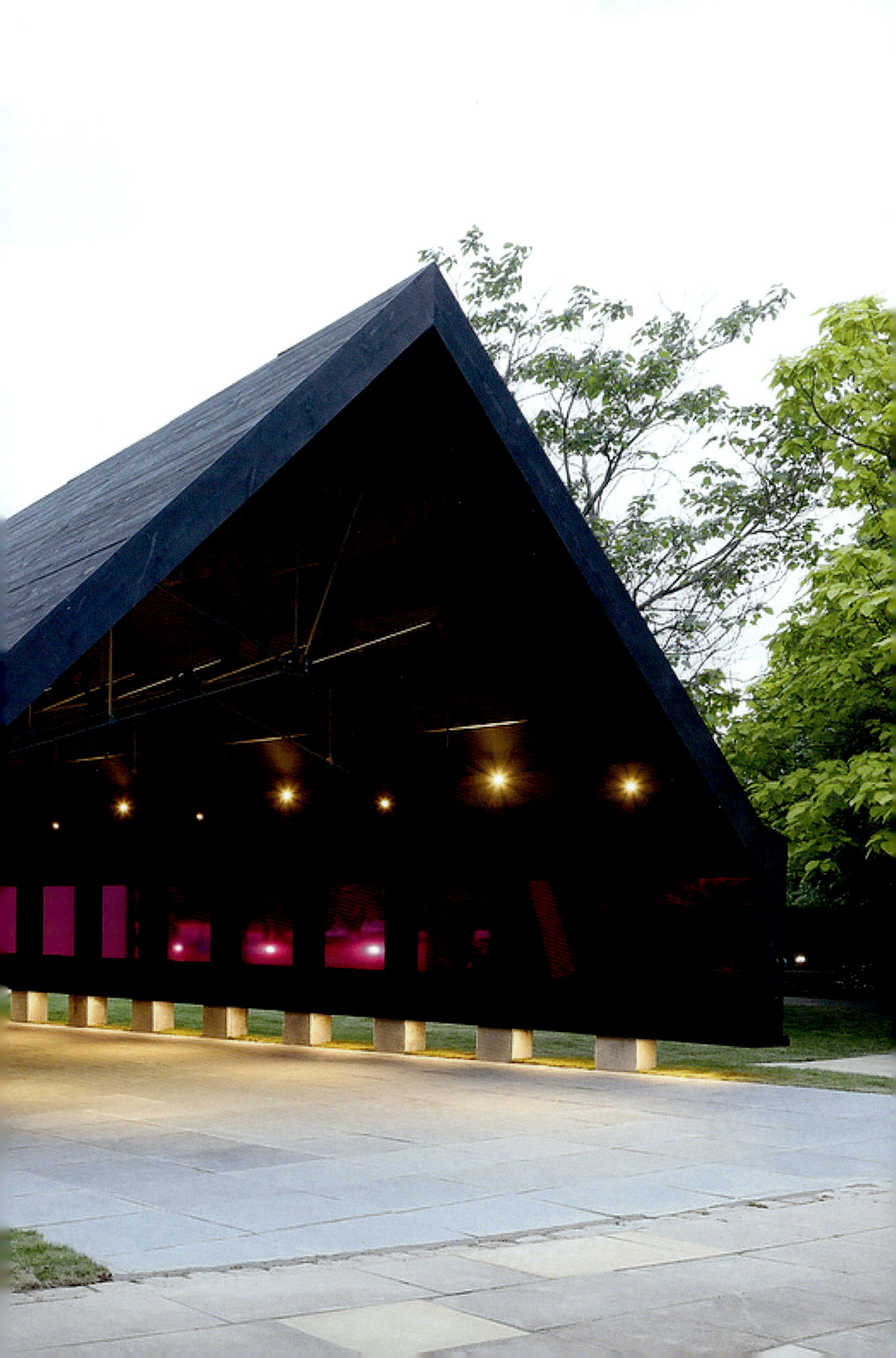

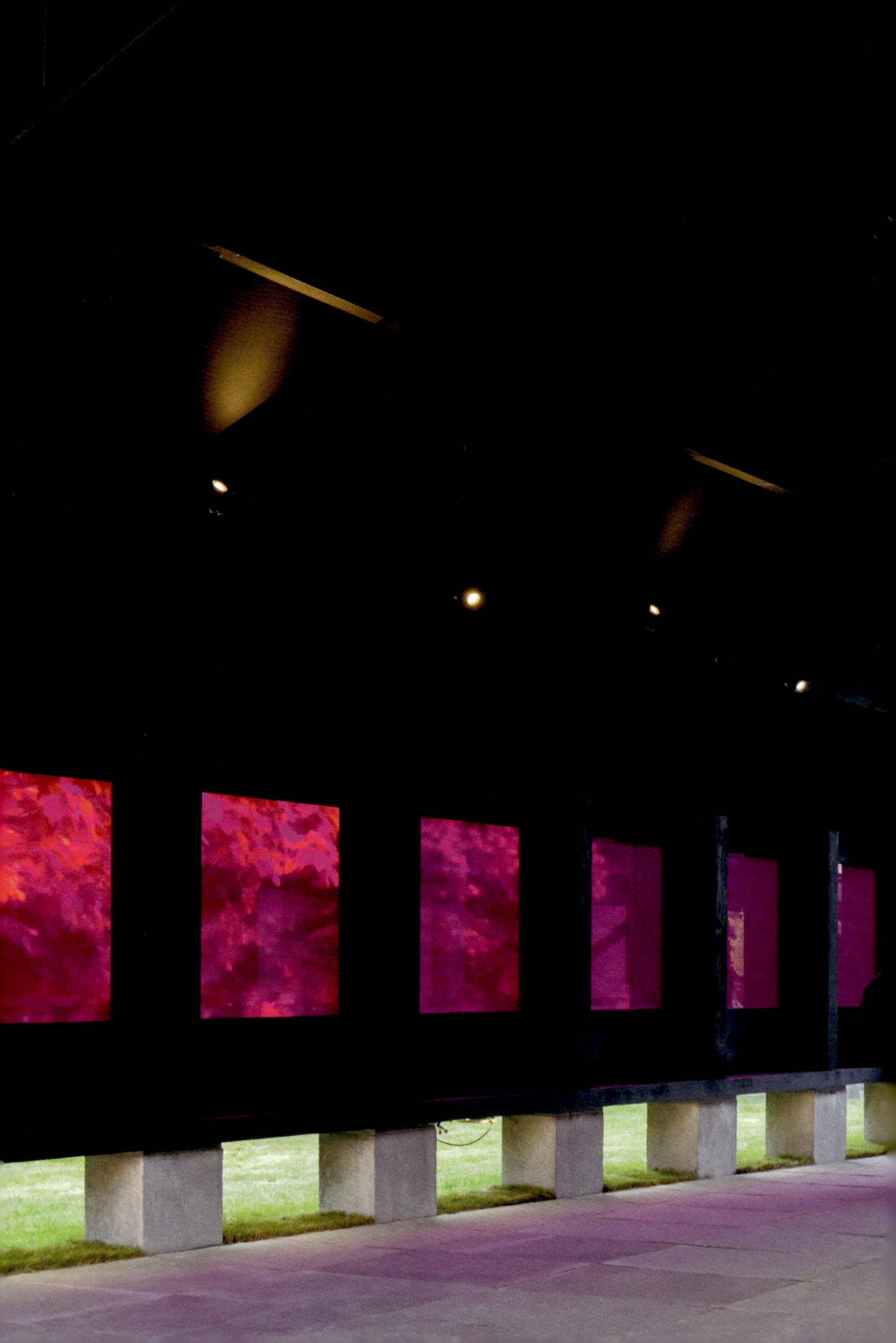

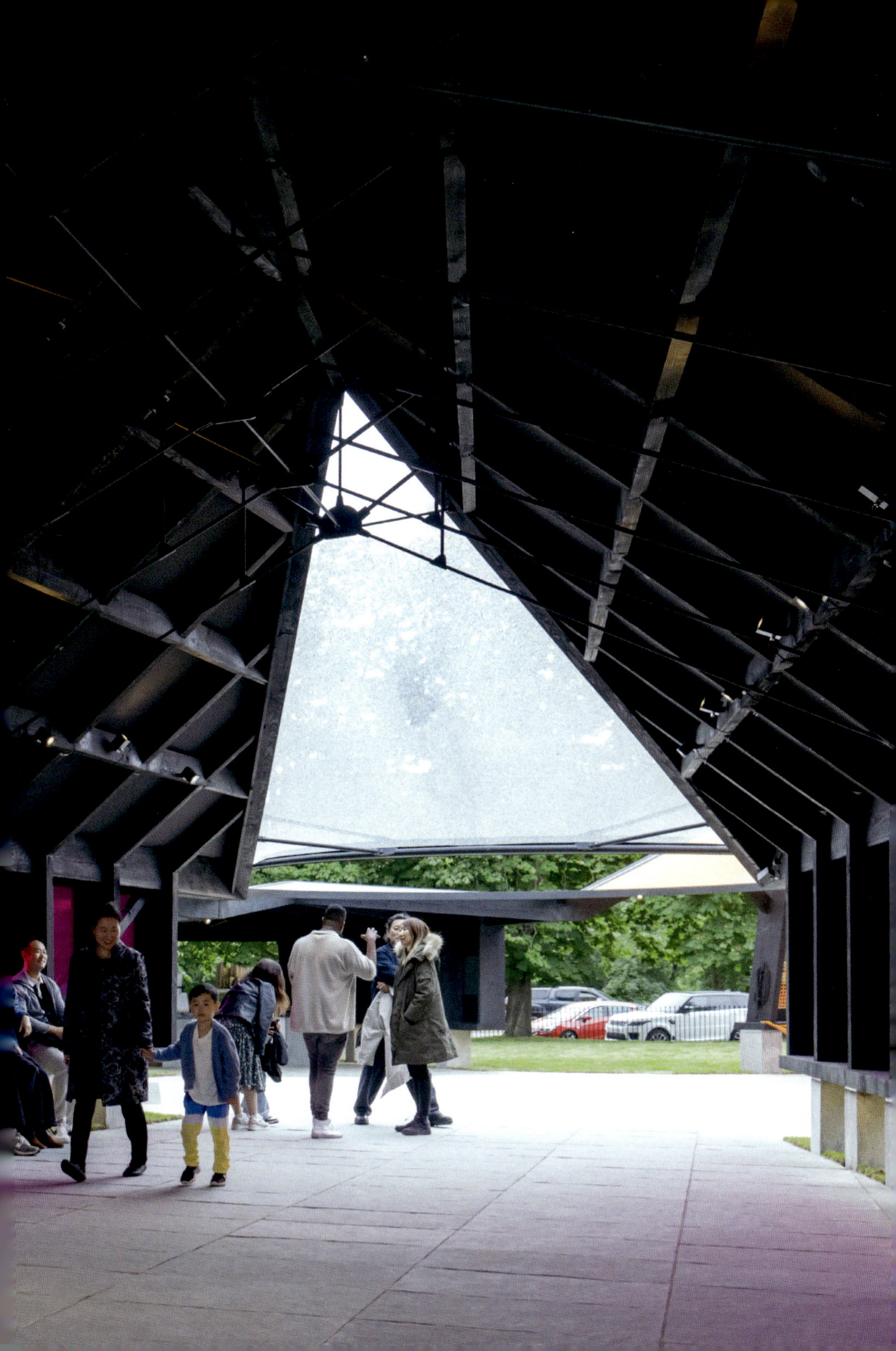

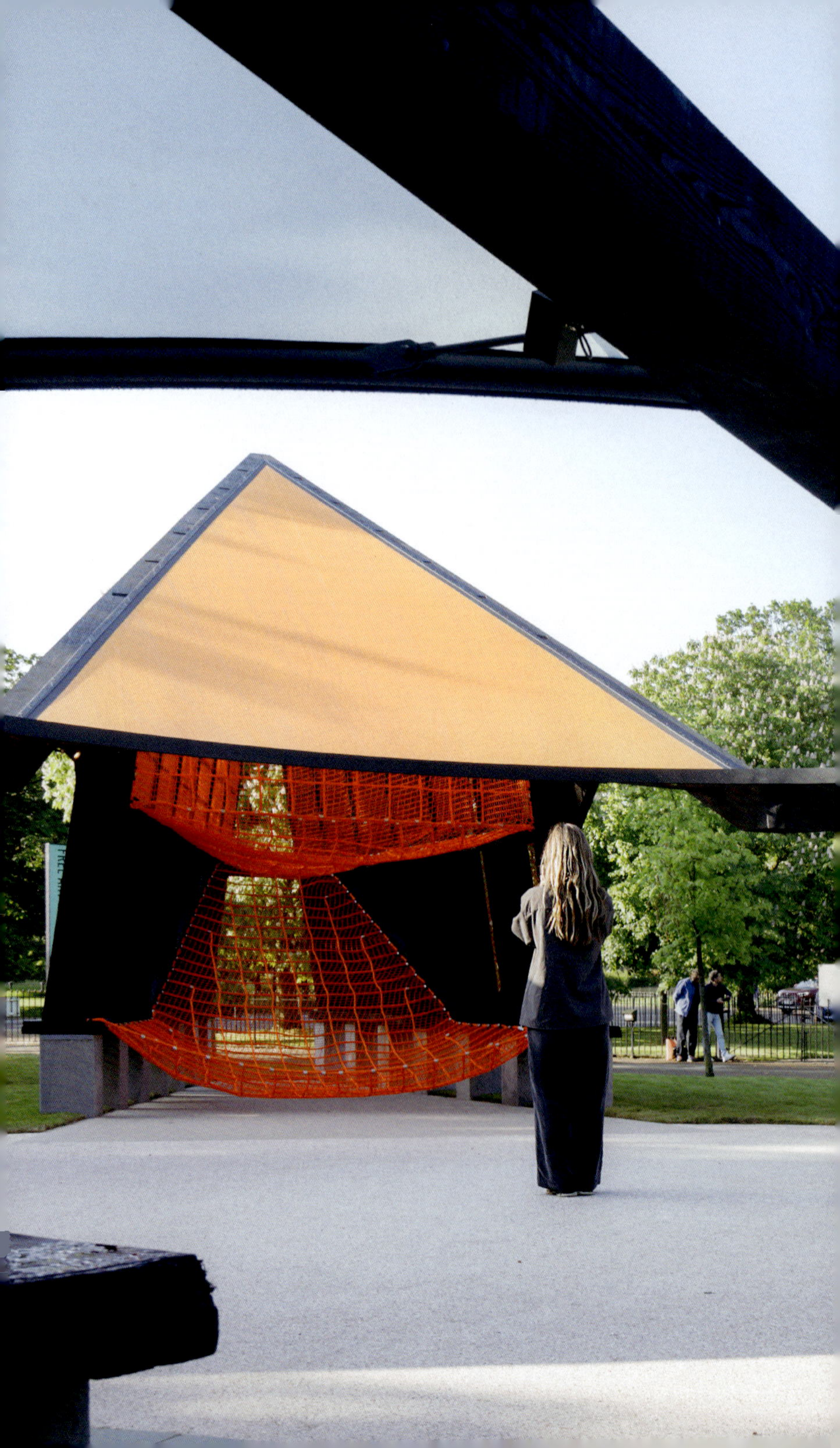

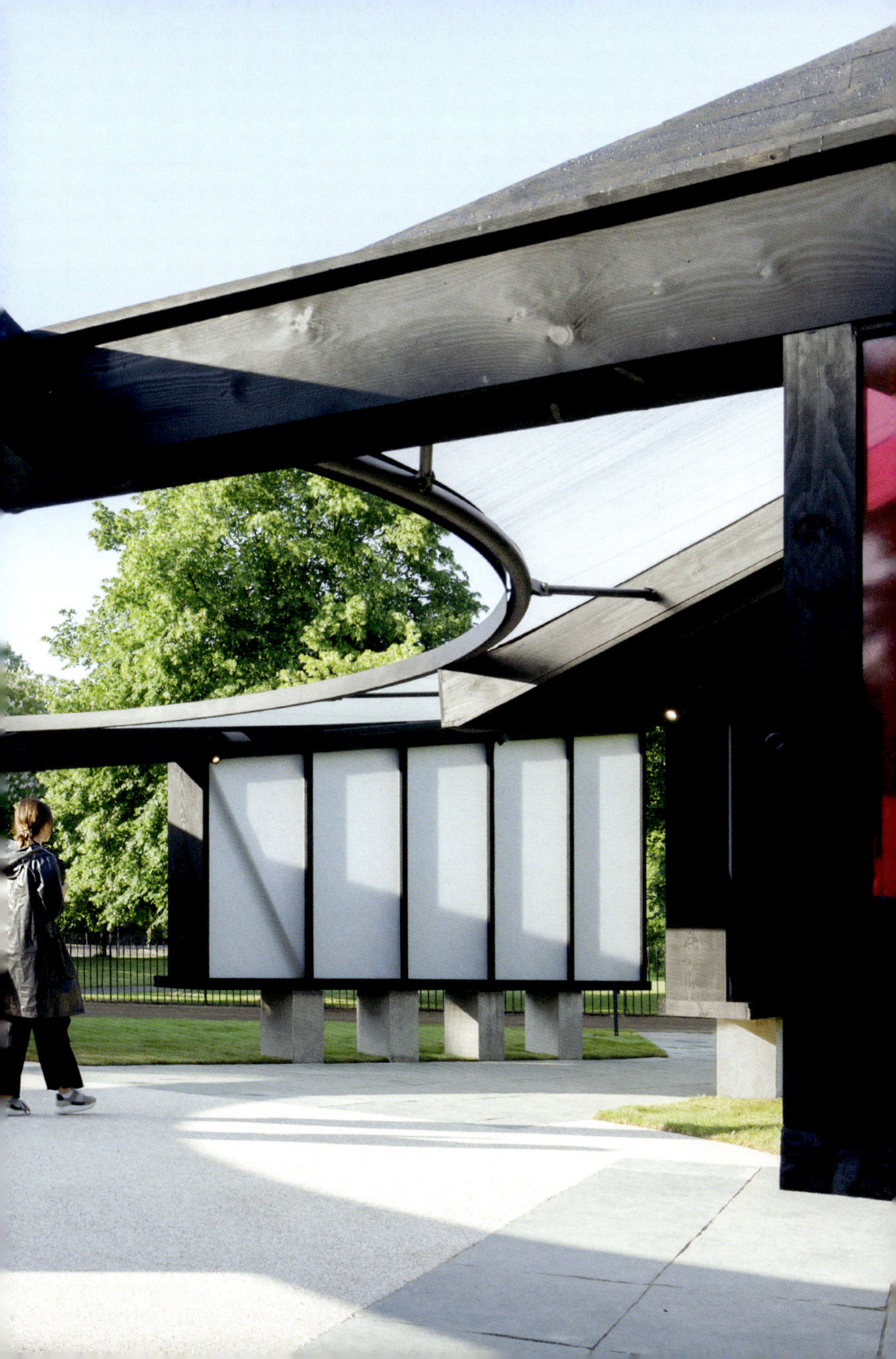

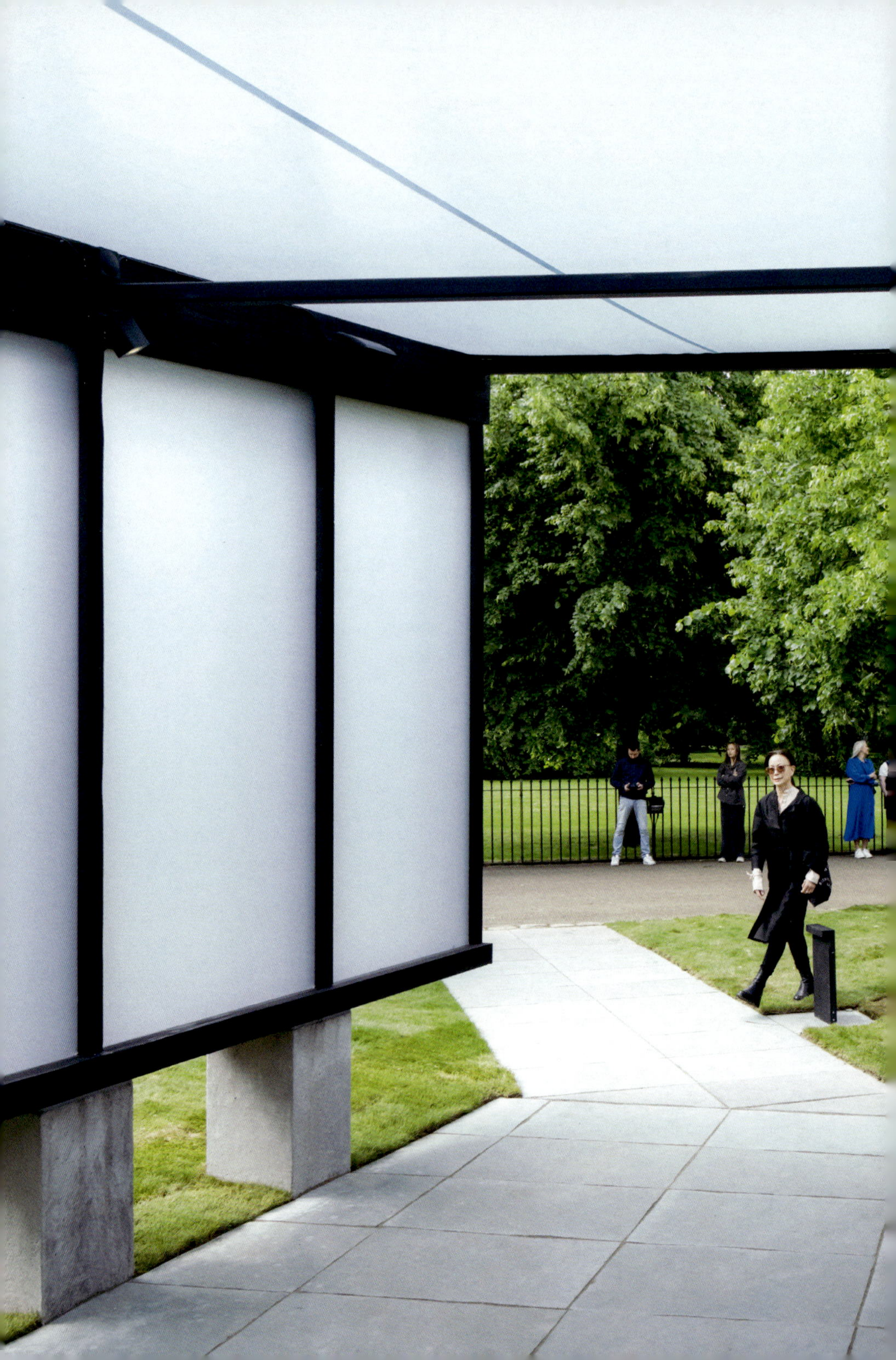

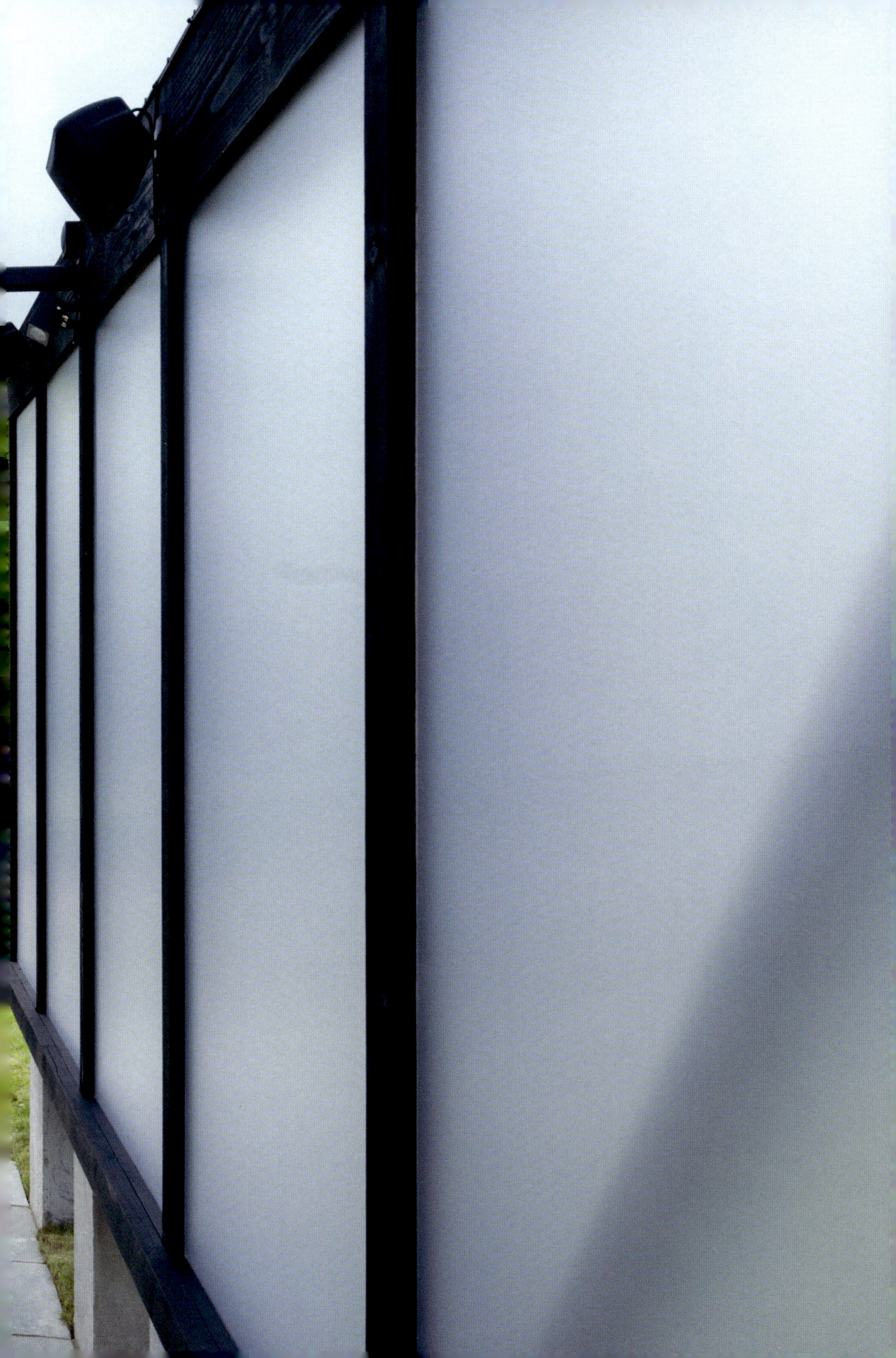

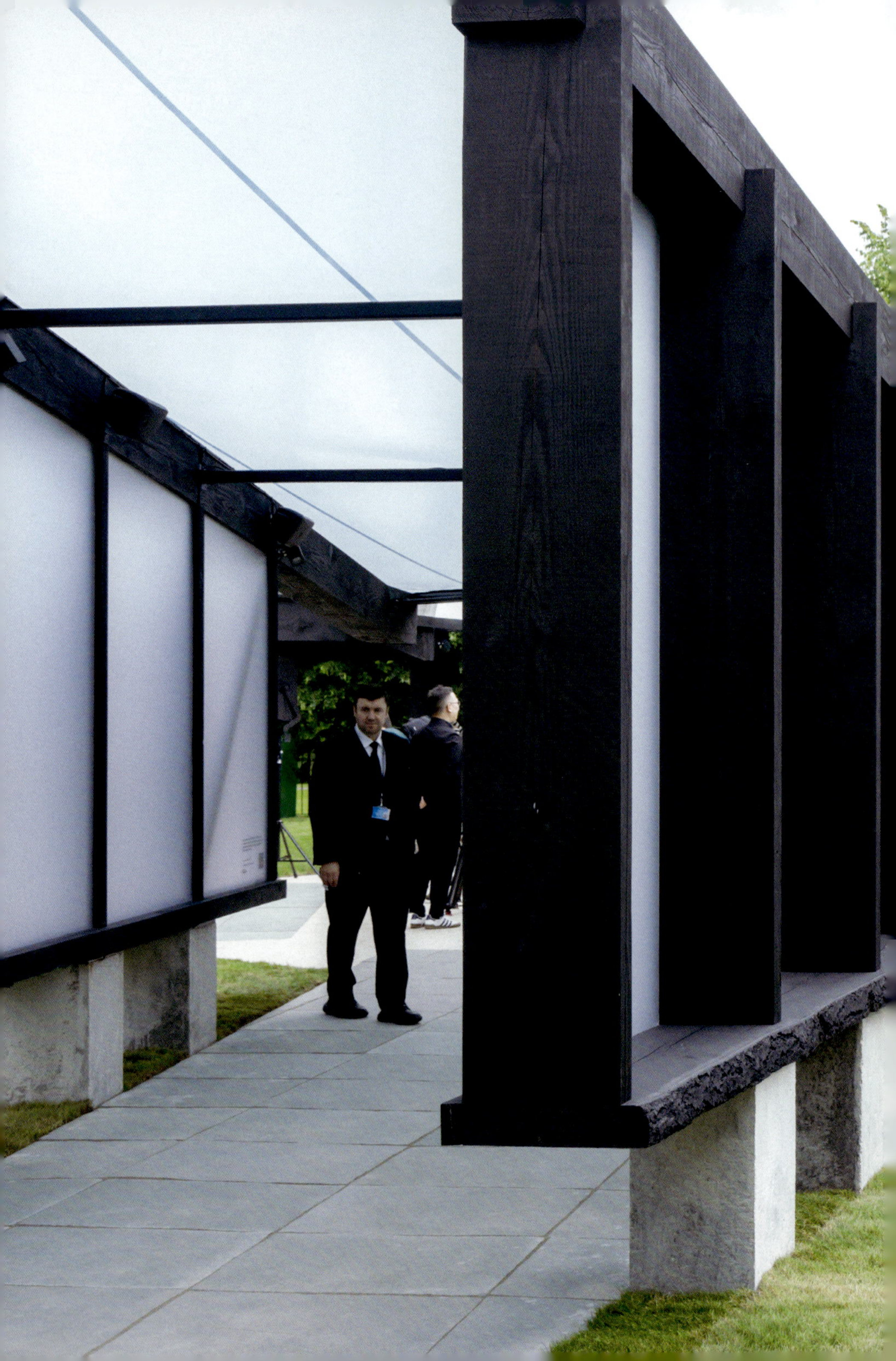

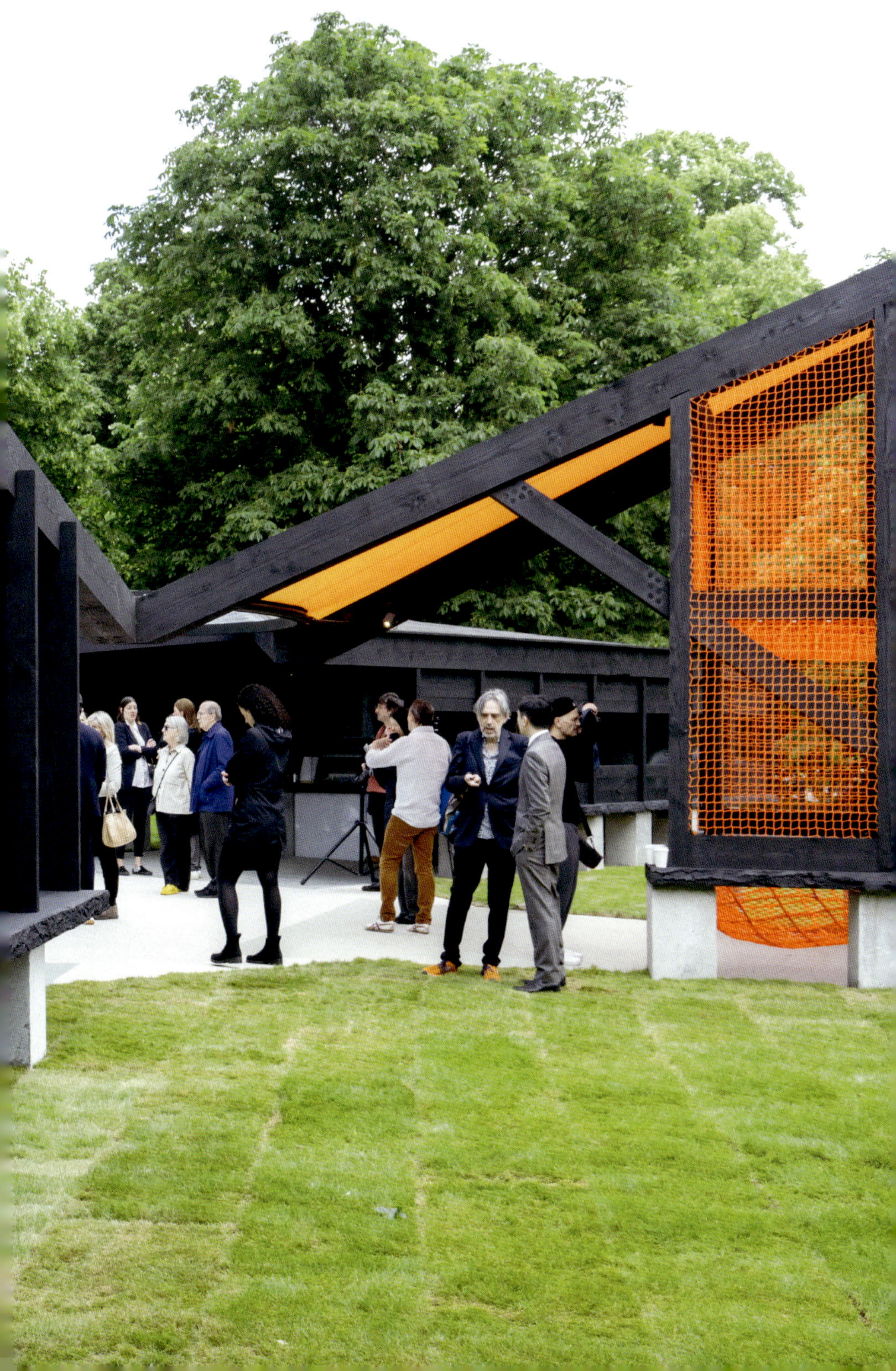

This catalogue is published to accompany the Serpentine Pavilion 2024 *Archipelagic Void* designed by Minsuk Cho, Mass Studies, 7 June–27 October 2024

Serpentine Pavilion 2024
© Minsuk Cho, Mass Studies

Edited by Alexa Chow, Gonzalo Herrero Delicado and Yesomi Umolu
Copyedited by Melissa Larner
Translation from Korean by Emily Jungmin Yoon
Designed by Sulki & Min
Printed by Gomer Press in Wales, UK

First published in 2024 by Serpentine and Verlag der Buchhandlung Walther und Franz König, Köln

© 2024 Minsuk Cho, Mass Studies; Serpentine, London; the authors; and Verlag der Buchhandlung Walther und Franz König, Köln

All rights reserved. No part of this publication may be reproduced, stored in a retrieval system or transmitted in any form or by any means, electronic, mechanical, photocopying, recording or otherwise without prior permission of the publishers. The publishers of this book are committed to respecting the intellectual property rights of others. Every effort has been made to trace copyright holders and to obtain their permission for the use of copyright material. The publishers apologise for any errors or omissions in the above list and would be grateful if notified of any corrections that should be incorporated in future reprints or editions of this book.

Published by

SERPENTINE

Serpentine
Kensington Gardens
London W2 3XA
Telephone +44 (0) 207 402 6075
Fax +44 (0) 207 402 4103
www.serpentinegalleries.org

Verlag der Buchhandlung Walther und Franz Konig
Ehrenstr. 4
D-50672 Köln

Bibliographic information published by the Deutsche Nationalbibliothek. The Deutsche National-bibliothek lists this publication in the Deutsche Nationalbibliografie; detailed bibliographic data are available on the Internet at http://dnb.d-nb.de.

Distribution

Europe
Buchhandlung Walther König
Ehrenstr. 4
D-50672 Köln
Telephone +49 (0) 221 / 20 59 6 53
verlag@buchhandlung-walther-koenig.de

UK & Ireland
ART DATA
12 Bell Industrial Estate
50 Cunningham Street
London W4 5HB
United Kingdom
Telephone +44 (0)208 747 10 61
Fax +44 (0)208 742 23 19
orders@artdata.co.uk

Outside Europe
D.A.P. / Distributed Art Publishers, Inc.
75 Broad Street, Suite 630
USA – New York, NY 10004
Telephone +1 (0) 212 627 1999
orders@dapinc.com

ISBN 978-1-908617-86-6
Serpentine, London

ISBN 978-3-7533-0688-9
Verlag der Buchhandlung
Walther und Franz König, Köln

Serpentine Pavilion 2024
Archipelagic Void
Mass Studies

Reflections

Serpentine Pavilion 2024 Archipelagic Void   Mass Studies

Edited by
Alexa Chow, Gonzalo Herrero Delicado
and Yesomi Umolu

Reflections

Kenneth Frampton   The Work of Minsuk Cho's Mass Studies, 2018–24   2

Stefano Boeri   Circular Mass   16

Kim Hyesoon   Glass Pavilion in the Ear   22

Heman Chong and Renée Staal   The Library of Unread Books   28

Kenneth Frampton
The Work of Minsuk Cho's Mass Studies, 2018–24

The spectacular Serpentine Pavilion 2024 is designed by the distinguished Korean architect Minsuk Cho, founder and principal of an architectural studio known by the evocative yet somehow misleading name, Mass Studies. This practice first fully demonstrated its prowess in an ingeniously rational dormitory complex designed and realised for Daejeon University in 2018. This work, faced throughout in traditional Korean black brick, was an exceptionally ingenious response to the challenge of building on a steeply sloping site in the context of a renowned residential college. Organised around a 5.4 square-metre room module that provides sleeping/working accommodation for four students each, the multi-storey complex is divided at mid-point by a communal floor, floating over an access road below, accommodating a restaurant and lounges, etc. This divides the dormitory complex into two, with male students occupying the bottom four floors of the complex on a precipitous site, descending a virtual cliff face, and female students occupying the upper four floors in partial stepped formation above; the two genders meet at the mid-point communal floors.

    Led by Minsuk Cho, the practice would follow this contextual and sectional triumph by beginning to work on the reconstruction and addition to the

Daejeon University
Residential College, 2018,
in Daejeon, South Korea.
Photo by Kyungsub Shin

French Embassy in Korea, reconstruction and addition, 2023, in Seoul, South Korea. Photo by Yong-Kwan Kim

French Embassy compound, originally completed in 1961 to the designs of the architect Kim Chung-up in a Neo-Corbusian manner, which he had acquired when working for the Franco-Swiss master in the 1950s. Mass Studies and the Paris-based Korean-French architect, Yoon Tae-hoon, would collaborate on restoring and adding to the compound, and the design of the ten-storey office tower. Its elegant, well-proportioned, light-weight, welded square-tubular steel frame, with black, prefabricated reinforced concrete infill panels combined with dark wood-patterned UHPC (ultra-high performance concrete) inserts henceforth became a characteristic syntax of the office. This virtually dematerialised dark tower would contrast in a self-effacing way with the robust reinforced concrete symbolic pavilion, capped, as in the original, by a carefully restored version of Kim Chung-up's cantilevered, butterfly roof.

    This major achievement was followed by a 2019 commission to restore and expand the Osulloc Tea Museum, situated in a bucolic landscape of tea plantations in the midst of the Gotjawal ecosystem of Jeju Island. Mass Studies was continually involved in this endeavour from 2011 onwards, beginning with the Tea Stone, Innisfree House and Annex of 2012 and going on to extend the Innisfree House in 2019 and finally to renovate and expand the existing Tea Museum in 2023. To accomplish this markedly *paysagiste* complex, Minsuk Cho was assisted by the landscape architect Jung Youngsun, and their

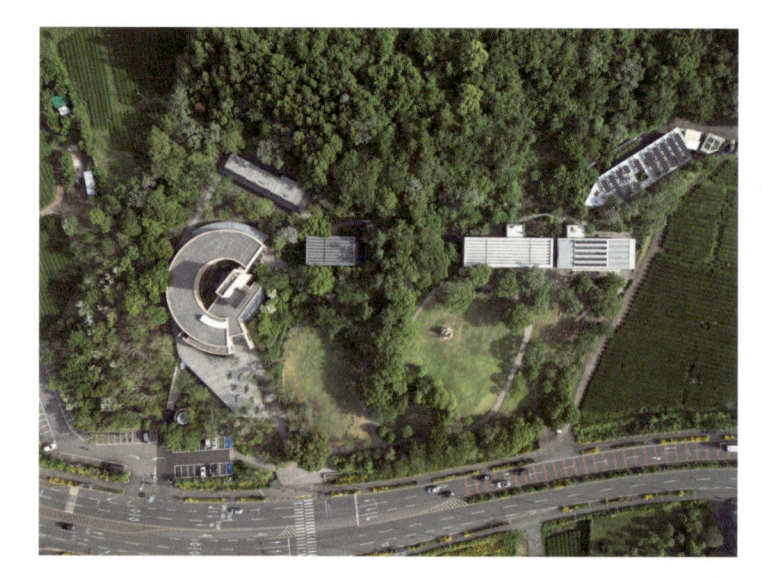

Osulloc Tea Museum
Extension, 2011–2023,
in Jeju Island, South Korea.
Photo by Taehee Cho

Osulloc Tea Factory, 2023,
in Jeju Island, Korea.
Photo by Yong-Kwan Kim

descriptive account of the overall intention behind the design can hardly be improved upon. They write:

> Visitors can explore interconnected, web-like 'paths', facilitating the discovery of relationships throughout the complex. These paths, varying in elevation, width, and contour, encourage movement and moments of pause, seamlessly blending nature and architecture. Transitioning from forested trails to interior passageways, visitors encounter a fluid experience that adapts to the terrain [...] The journey unfolds amidst vast, bright green tea plantations and intimate shaded, Gotjawal forests.

Apart from the renovation and extension of the cylindrical Tea Museum in 2023, the overall assembly comprises a series of single-storey, steel-framed, open-plan buildings, each one devoted to refreshments, combined with the tasting and selling of green tea. Since these are glazed from floor to ceiling, the clientele are perennially exposed to the bucolic landscape on all sides. This enclave is complemented by the nearby Osulloc Tea Factory, realised to designs of the same architects in 2023, a long, two-storey high, concrete-framed production space, with mezzanines throughout its length, designed for the processing, packaging and storage of tea. Tourists are again provided with viewing windows through which they can witness segments of the production.

Choru, 2023, in Boseong, South Jeolla Province, South Korea. Photo by Yong-Kwan Kim

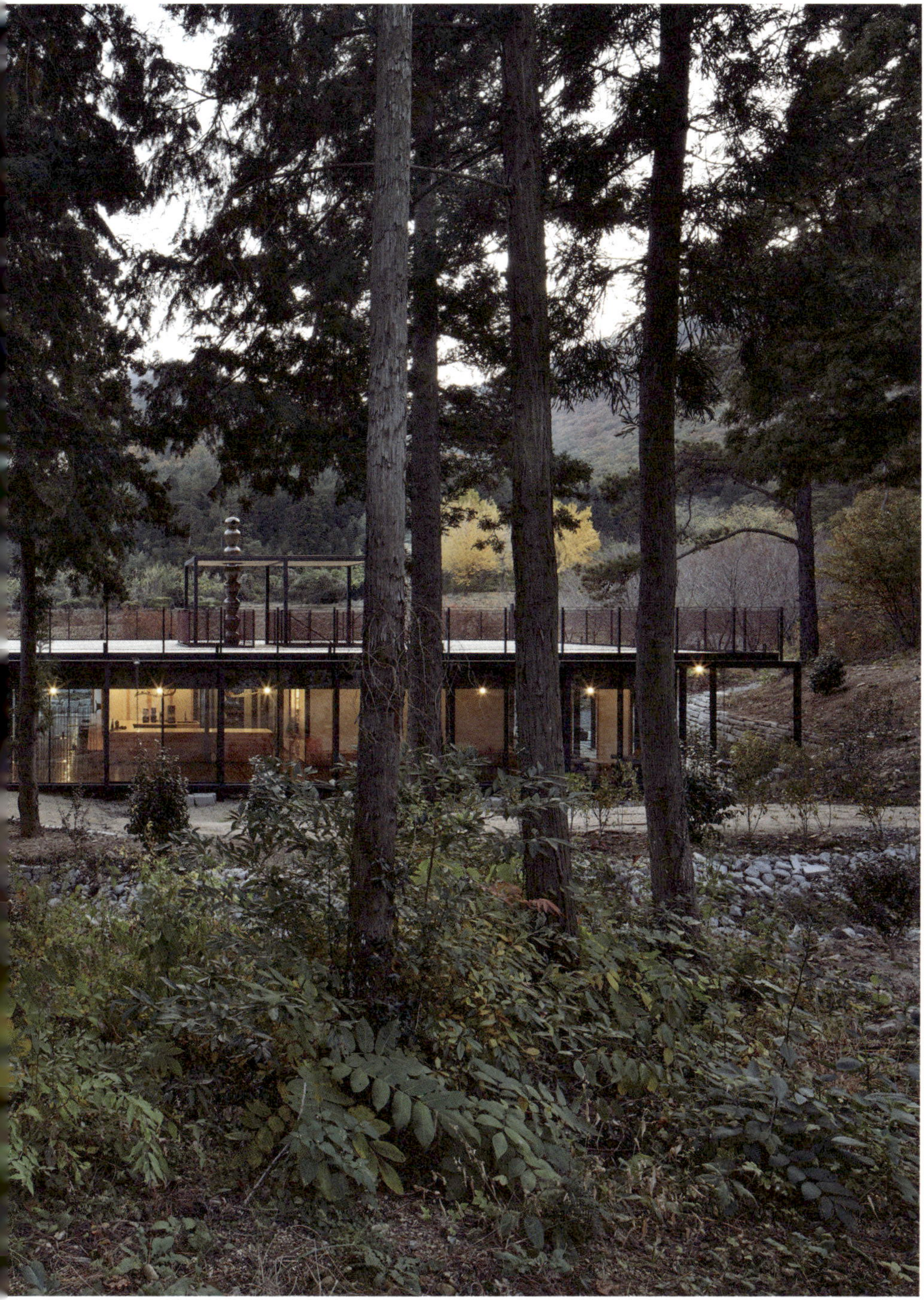

In 2020, Mass Studies started to work on yet another facility associated with traditional Korean gastronomic culture, namely, the production of black vinegar. Located close to Haepyeongho Lake in the forested Obongsan Mountain Valley, the building is an eight by five bay, single-storey, steel-framed café space, elevated above an uneven site. It is accessed through a rooftop patio via a light steel bridge from a higher part of the site. This exceptionally calm space sets itself up as an ideal environment in which tourists may savour delectable beverages made out of black vinegar. The quasi-religious space with sliding-folding screens and ceilings lined with plywood has the uncanny atmosphere of a domestic domain rather than a café. Ringed with rough stone paving taken from a nearby quarry and adjacent to a stream from which it is protected by a stone earthwork, the café looks over fields filled with *onggi* jars, within which the vinegar is fermented. These black jars, handmade by Korean master ceramicist Lee Haksoo, are exhibited everywhere throughout the café and have also been assembled by the architect into a chimney passing up through the entry patio. In many respects this work may be seen as exemplifying the structural *lingua franca* of the office, namely, thin welded, light-weight, orthogonal framing in square-tubular steel.

The most significant work of the practice to be realised in the Korean capital to date is unquestionably the Won Buddhism Wonnam Temple, designed and realised between 2018 and 2022. The main *dharma* building of the temple complex

Won Buddhism Wonnam
Temple, 2022, in
Seoul, South Korea.
Photo by Kyungsub Shin

Won Buddhism Wonnam
Temple, 2022, in
Seoul, South Korea.
Photo by Kyungsub Shin

is the so-called Won Space within the sanctuary, rendered sacrosanct by a circle 7.4 metre in diameter cut out from a nine metre tall surface, the top-lit world image to which the congregation is focused. The entire structure, including its ancillary social facilities, is of reinforced concrete construction, which is treated as a continuous, highly expressive plastic form, woven into the interstitial fabric of the historical centre of Seoul; inserted quite literally into an irregular, 'left-over' space. A loose fit, so to speak, between the form and space has enabled the architects to create a labyrinth of alleyways so as to maintain pedestrian circulation throughout the site, providing access to adjacent properties on either side. Of equally sacred status as the inner sanctum is a small open-air patio between the temple and a Korean *hanok*, fabricated in the traditional manner out of heavy timber. This free-standing, honorific structure is the Inhyewon Donor Memorial.

Despite its relatively light-weight, temporary, timber-framed presence, the Serpentine Pavilion designed by Minsuk Cho is as worldly as the Wonnam Temple in its universal significance, including the circular 'left-over' void formed by the eaves of the five independent structures from which it is composed. This anti-pavilion is made up from a central, precise but ephemeral circle, subtended in space, like all the other temporary pavilions designed by the office in the two decades of its existence. According to the architect, this is the 'archipelagic void', a concept derived from the poet and philosopher Édouard

Glissant's *The Archipelago Conversations* (2022), which is a record of an exchange with Hans Ulrich Obrist, giving this year's pavilion an intimate touch.

The Pavilion is comprised of five timber-framed, single-storey, 'open-air', spread-eagled structures, the central axes of which are oriented towards five different destinations: the *Auditorium* towards Serpentine South, the *Library* towards Paddington Station, the *Tea House* towards the Princess Diana memorial, the *Play Tower* towards Buckingham Palace and the *Gallery* towards the Albert Memorial. Each of these structures seems to have its own implicit cultural/transcultural affinity, the first one alluding to discourse, the second to literacy, the third to the culture of tea, the fourth to the irrepressible energy of the young and the fifth to the ever diminishing potential of fine art.

The central, implicitly cylindrical, empty volume alludes to the courtyard or *madang* of the traditional Korean house as a versatile space capable of accommodating a range of diverse purposes. Additionally, the elevation of the prefabricated timber-framing on concrete blocks throughout not only makes reference to the universal vernacular of raising timber granaries on stone plinths, but also induces an aerial floating character, reminiscent of Kasimir Melnikov's USSR Pavilion erected for the Exposition des Arts Decoratifs, staged in Paris in 1925, evoking the *zaum*, transrational, agitational spirit of the Soviet avant garde in the 1920s.

Seyeonjeong Pavilion,
c. 1637, Bogildo Island,
Wando County, South Jeolla
Province, South Korea.
Photo by Minsuk Cho

Kenneth Frampton trained as an architect at the Architectural Association School of Architecture, London. From 1972 until 2019 he served as Ware Professor of Architecture at the Graduate School of Architecture, Planning and Preservation, Columbia University, New York. He is the author of numerous essays and books on modern and contemporary architecture, including *Studies in Techtonic Culture* (2001), *Labour, Work, and Architecture* (2002), *Modern Architecture: A Critical History* (2007) and *A Genealogy of Modern Architecture* (2015).

Stefano Boeri
Circular Mass

In 2008 in Milan, we needed a luminescent diamond.

A sparkling and permeable space was required to host a series of conversations organised by the magazine *Abitare* for the seventh edition of Milan Design Week, *FuoriSalone*. The event would take place within one of Milan's most iconic arcades, the Galleria Vittorio Emanuele II — the commercial arcade that connects Piazza del Duomo with Piazza della Scala.

I knew the work of Mass Studies and Minsuk Cho well, and I had visited a few weeks earlier, with architect and critic Joseph Grima, the dome constructed from white hula-hoops that Minsuk had created in front of the Storefront for Art and Architecture's headquarters in Manhattan to celebrate its 25th anniversary.

But in the Galleria in Milan, the challenge was more difficult. It was not just a matter of creating a pavilion in a square, but of realising a void within a void, making the space of the pavilion a discrete entity, yet capable of being both permeable and welcoming.

The Ring Dome designed by Mass Studies, proved ideal for the task. With a diameter of approximately 8 metres and built with 1,500 hula-hoops and 12,000 cable ties, it hosted conversations between Hans Ulrich Obrist, Pierre Paulin and Rem Koolhaas and fifty participants including Naoto Fukasawa, Gaetano Pesce and Oliviero Toscani, along with a day-long open editorial meeting.

The most interesting aspect of Cho's Ring Dome project was its strong typology of space that on the one hand could become an intimate and protected place, and on the other remained porous and open to the lights and noises of the context in which it was situated.

Ring Dome, 2008, in Milan, Italy.
Photo by Eric Xu and Vivi YingHo

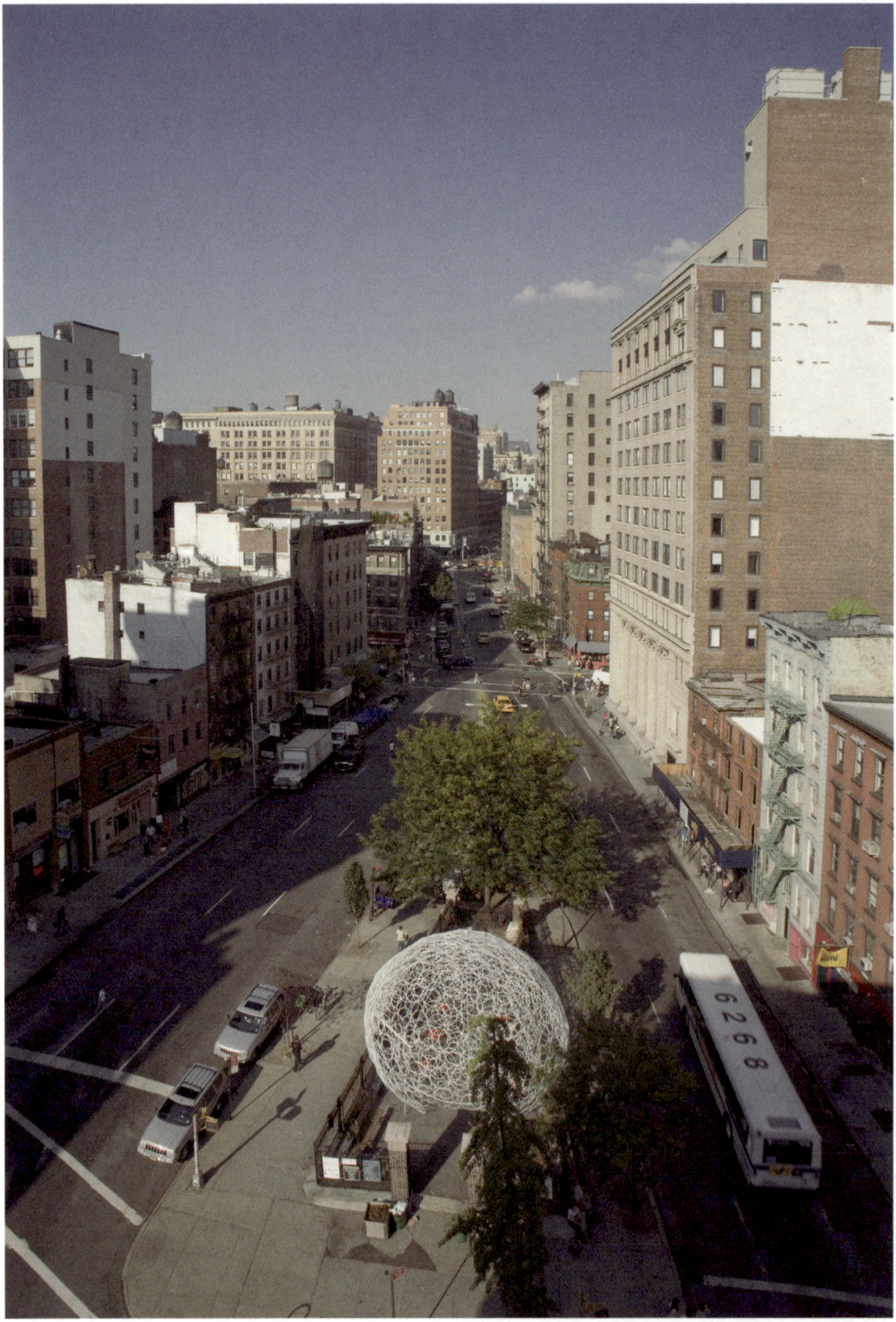
6268

It should not come as a surprise that the original idea behind the design was for a collective celebration of life, inspired by the *Burning Man* festival. The Ring Dome's pure and vibrant form was conceived as a 'variable geometry' through the multiplication of a minimal element, and this clear formal concept was therefore capable of adapting to different places. Ring Dome moved from New York to Kitakyushu, then to Milan and Seoul, among other places in the world, and every time it was built and dismantled, it produced a popular spectacle. The luminescent white plastic hula hoops were assembled together according to a very simple scheme by artists and citizens, and distributed as toys to all participants after disassembly.

Ring Dome, 2007, in New York City, USA.
Photo by Gaia Cambiaggi

Stefano Boeri is an architect and urban planner. He is Professor at Politecnico di Milano and Director of the Future City Lab at Tongji University, Shanghai. His work ranges from planning, architecture and urban visions to design, with a constant focus on the geopolitical and environmental implications of urban phenomena. He designed the Bosco Verticale (2014) in Milan, Italy, and is among the leading players in the international debates on climate change and architecture. In 2018, he was appointed President of Triennale Milano, one of world's leading cultural institutions, conveying the complexities of the contemporary world in a host of artistic forms: design, architecture and the visual, scenic and performing arts.

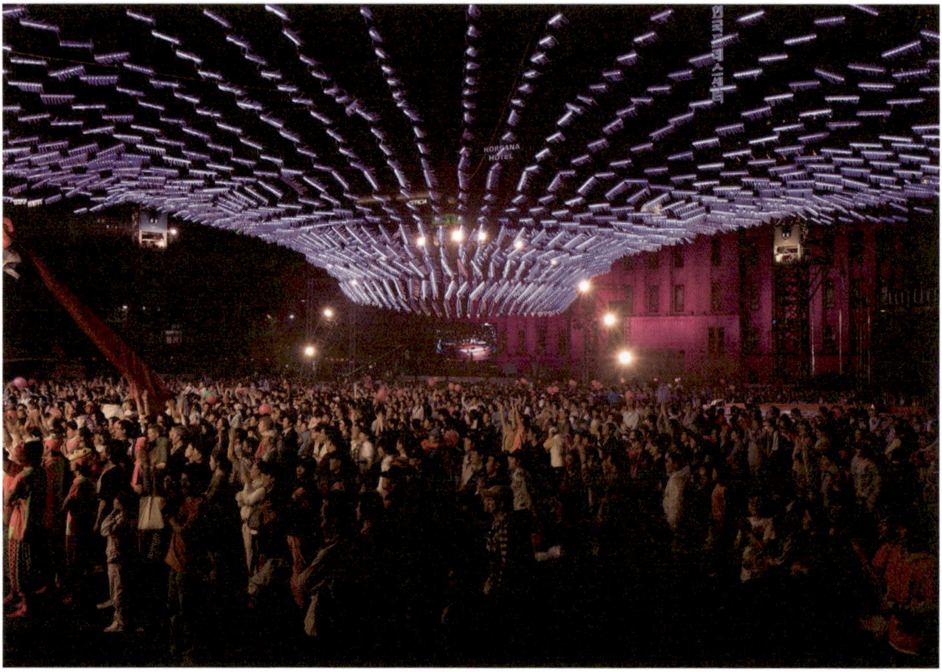

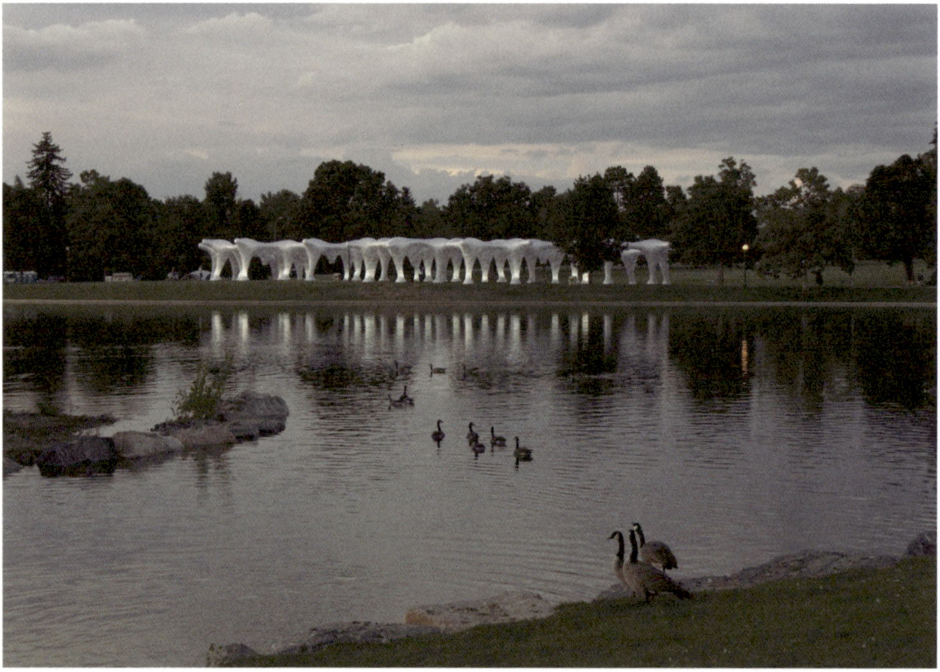

May Palace, 2008, in Seoul, South Korea, as part of the HiSeoul Festival directed by Eun-Me Ahn. Photo by Yong-Kwan Kim

Air Forest, 2008, in Denver, CO, USA, as part of Dialog:City, during the Democratic National Convention. Photo by Jason Walp

Open Pavilion, 2010, in Anyang, South Korea, as part of the 2010 Anyang Public Art Project directed by Kyong Park. Photo by Kyungsub Shin

Vacant House, 2010, in Sajik Park, Gwangju, South Korea. Photo by Iwan Baan

Rendering of the Hyper Pavilion, at the Danginri Cultural Power Plant (under construction), in Seoul, South Korea. Image by Mass Studies

김혜순
귓속의 유리정자

나는 상상한다.
바람으로 지은 건축.
빛으로 지은 건축.
미소로 지은 건축.

할아버지의 괘종시계로 들어간 기분일까?
괘종시계는 5인승 자전거처럼 꾸벅꾸벅 공원을 달릴 수 있을까?

아니면 부채 속 같을까?
거인이 부채를 들고 펄렁펄렁 부치면
그 안에 노래하는 사람들과 춤추는 사람들이 공원에 나타날까?
누워있는 대관람차 속 같을까, 그 곳에서 당신을 바라볼까, 창밖을 내다볼까.

그것도 아니면 우주를 떠가는 배 같을까?
신기루 같을까? 노스탤지어 같을까? 별빛 같을까?
그 배들에는 방향키가 없는 것 같을 거다.
정박한 것인지 표류하는 것인지 알 수 없을 거다.

더 다가가서 보면 '바퀴인가해시계인가섬인가풍차인가깍지낀손인가', 즐거운 상상.
나는 다섯 번째 칸에서 쉴게요, 중얼거려 보지만 어디나 다섯 번째 칸일 거다.

Kim Hyesoon
Glass Pavilion in the Ear

I picture it:
Architecture by wind.
Architecture by light.
Architecture by smiles.

Entering it — would it feel like stepping inside Grandpa's grandfather clock?
Would this grandfather clock nod and drift off, through
    the gardens, like a five-person bike?

Or would it be like the inside of a folding fan?
If a giant were to lift and flutter the fan,
would its singers and dancers appear in the gardens?
Would it be like the inside of a Ferris wheel, laid flat? From there,
    shall I peer out at you, or the window?

If none of those — would it be like a ship, drifting away from the galaxy?
And what would that be like — a mirage? Nostalgia? Starlight?
There would be no ship's wheel on such a vessel.
There would be no way to know whether the ship were anchored or adrift.

Upon a closer look: a wheel-or-sundial-or-island-or-windmill-
    or-hands-intertwined. A fun thought.
I'll unwind in the fifth island, I mumble, but of course, every cell is the fifth one.

가운데 허공을 두어야만 굴러가는 하늘위의 저 밝은 동그라미처럼
'바퀴인가해시계인가섬인가풍차인가깍지낀손인가'가 나보다 몇 걸음 앞서 달려갈 거다.

'바퀴인가해시계인가섬인가풍차인가깍지낀손인가'가 작은 허공처럼 떨다가.
엎드린 나의 척추를 하나하나 짚고 올라올 거다.
내 귓속으로 들어와 유리정자를 지을 거다.
귓속 정자에서는 시인이 바퀴와 해시계와 섬과 풍차와 깍지 낀 두 손의 한가운데엔
텅 빈 허공이 있다고 시를 읽어줄 거다.
그 시가 입김으로 나를 간질일지도 몰라.

나는 그 시인을 안아줄 거다.
그러면 신이 땅 위에 **뼈**를 늘어놓고 그 위에 구름을 덮은 것처럼
'바퀴인가해시계인가섬인가풍차인가깍지낀손인가'의 건축이 내 안에서 갈비**뼈**처럼 펴질 거다.
그것의 체온이 내게로 전해질 거다.

나는 건축물에게도 체온이 있다, 라고 생각한다.

그러자 내 안에 사람들이 가득 들어찬 듯
노래하고 춤추는 소리 몸통을 둥둥 울릴 거다.
나를 건축하는 슬픔이 몸통을 둥둥 울릴 거다.

나는 또 상상한다.
허공으로 지은 건축.
구름으로 지은 건축.
음악으로 지은 건축.

Like that brilliant ring in the sky, that can only
    revolve with the void in its middle,
the wheel-or-sundial-or-island-or-windmill-or-hands-intertwined
    will run a few paces ahead of me.

The wheel-or-sundial-or-island-or-windmill-or-hands-intertwined
    will tremble, like a little void.
Then, it will climb my folded back, one vertebra at a time.
It will come into my ear, build a glass pavilion.
In the ear pavilion, a poet will read a poem: in the middle of
    the wheel, sundial, island, two intertwined hands,
there is an empty void.
Maybe that poem will tickle me with its breath.

I will embrace that poet.
Then, as if a god has spread bones on the earth
    and covered them with clouds,
the architecture of the wheel-or-sundial-or-island-or-windmill-
    or-hands-intertwined will unwind, open like a ribcage.
I will sense its body heat.

A piece of architecture has body heat, too, I think.

Then, as if people have filled my insides,
the sounds of song and dance will reverberate in my torso.
The sadness that constructs who I am will reverberate in my torso.

Once again, I picture it:
Architecture by void.
Architecture by cloud.
Architecture by music.

빛 속에 흔들리는 거대한 단풍잎 하나.
잎맥 따라 투명한 끈들처럼 빛이 흐르는 모듈의 빼곡한 얽힘.

박하사탕 같은 빛 속에서 자신의 유령을 벗어 나무에 거는 사람들.
입속이 환해지는 사람들.

저절로 주먹이 펴지는 손.

A single vast maple leaf, swaying in the light.
The dense intertwinement of modules, light flowing down
    the veins, as if they are transparent twine.

The people who shed their ghosts in the peppermint candy light
    to drape them on trees.
People whose mouths start to illuminate inside.

The fist that unfolds on its own.

Kim Hyesoon is a poet, essayist, and critic born in South Korea and based in Seoul. She has published fourteen poetry books, including *Autobiography of Death* (2018), *Phantom Pain of Wings* (2019) and essays including 'Do Womananimalasia' (2019). Her books have been translated into several languages, including eleven collections translated into English. She has received multiple international literature prizes, including the Griffin Poetry Prize (2019, Canada), Cikada Prize (2021, Sweden) and the National Book Critics Circle Award for poetry (2024, US). She has also received numerous literature awards in South Korea, most recently the Samsung Ho-Am Prize (2022). She is an Honorary Professor at the Seoul Institute of the Arts, where she taught creative writing for thirty-two years.

Heman Chong and Renée Staal
The Library of Unread Books

Heman Chong is an artist whose work is located at the intersection between image, performance and writing. Through interrogation and intervention, Chong investigates the function of everyday infrastructure as a political medium. He is currently working on solo shows at UCCA Dune (2024), Singapore Art Museum (2025) and Tai Kwun (2026). Together with Singapore-based collection manager **Renée Staal**, he co-founded *The Library of Unread Books* in 2016.

Located to the north of the Pavilion is *The Library of Unread Books* (2016–ongoing), an artwork by artist Heman Chong and archivist Renée Staal. This 'living' reference library, is comprised of donated unread books to form a pool of common knowledge, addressing notions of access, excess and the politics of distribution.

Back in 2016, we had the idea to create a public reference library composed of books sitting unread on the shelves of our friends. We quickly discovered that it is common to buy books without reading them immediately, and many of these books remain unread for a long time. We decided to ask our friends to donate these books so that someone else could read them.

By collecting and displaying books that people choose not to read, The Library of Unread Books makes a collective gesture addressing the circulation, distribution, access and surplus of knowledge. The books are always displayed haphazardly as stacks, defying any scientific system of organisation, so the library is always a chaotic mess. Every encounter is a surprise, not only for the reader but also for us.

We insist that our library functions like an epiphyte, growing on the surfaces of other institutions. We hope it will inspire these institutions to create common spaces for people to gather, common tools for people to use, and sustainable ways of working that do not exhaust resources or the possibility of community.

If you have a book to donate, please find us on Instagram and send us a direct message. We will provide instructions on where to send your unread book. We thank you deeply.

Heman Chong & Renée Staal

View of *The Library of Unread Books*, 2016–ongoing, by Heman Chong and Renée Staal, at the Serpentine Pavilion 2024. Photo by Iwan Baan

31

This catalogue is published
to accompany the
Serpentine Pavilion 2024
Archipelagic Void designed by
Minsuk Cho, Mass Studies,
7 June–27 October 2024

Serpentine Pavilion 2024
© Minsuk Cho, Mass Studies

Edited by Alexa Chow,
Gonzalo Herrero Delicado
and Yesomi Umolu
Copyedited by Melissa Larner
Translation from Korean by
Emily Jungmin Yoon
Designed by Sulki & Min
Printed by Gomer Press in
Wales, UK

First published in 2024 by
Serpentine and Verlag der
Buchhandlung Walther und
Franz König, Köln

© 2024 Minsuk Cho,
Mass Studies; Serpentine,
London; the authors;
and Verlag der Buchhandlung
Walther und Franz König, Köln

All rights reserved. No part
of this publication may
be reproduced, stored
in a retrieval system or
transmitted in any form or
by any means, electronic,
mechanical, photocopying,
recording or otherwise
without prior permission of
the publishers. The publishers
of this book are committed
to respecting the intellectual
property rights of others.
Every effort has been made
to trace copyright holders and
to obtain their permission for
the use of copyright material.
The publishers apologise
for any errors or omissions
in the above list and would
be grateful if notified of any
corrections that should be
incorporated in future reprints
or editions of this book.

Published by

SERPENTINE

Serpentine
Kensington Gardens
London W2 3XA
Telephone +44 (0) 207 402 6075
Fax +44 (0) 207 402 4103
www.serpentinegalleries.org

**Verlag der Buchhandlung
Walther und Franz Konig**
Ehrenstr. 4
D-50672 Köln

Bibliographic information
published by the Deutsche
Nationalbibliothek. The
Deutsche National-bibliothek
lists this publication in the
Deutsche Nationalbibliografie;
detailed bibliographic data are
available on the Internet at
http://dnb.d-nb.de.

Distribution

Europe
Buchhandlung Walther König
Ehrenstr. 4
D-50672 Köln
Telephone +49 (0) 221 / 20 59 6 53
verlag@buchhandlung-walther-koenig.de

UK & Ireland
ART DATA
12 Bell Industrial Estate
50 Cunnington Street
London W4 5HB
United Kingdom
Telephone +44 (0)208 747 10 61
Fax +44 (0)208 742 23 19
orders@artdata.co.uk

Outside Europe
D.A.P. / Distributed Art Publishers, Inc.
75 Broad Street, Suite 630
USA – New York, NY 10004
Telephone +1 (0) 212 627 1999
orders@dapinc.com

ISBN 978-1-908617-86-6
Serpentine, London

ISBN 978-3-7533-0688-9
Verlag der Buchhandlung
Walther und Franz König, Köln